Beyond
The Mayflower Steps

Joy Harvey

First published in Great Britain in 2020 by

Figtree Industries
3 Prospect Cottages
Snailbeach
Shrewsbury
SY5 0LR

ISBN 978-0-9572390-9-8

Edited by Figtree Industries
Designed and typeset in Cambria and Balqis by Figtree Industries
Cover design by Daniel Kevin Lloyd (www.danielkevinlloyd.com)
Produced by Figtree Industries (www.figtreeindustries.co.uk)
Printed by print2demand (www.print2demand.co.uk)

Dedication and Acknowledgements

This book is dedicated to Sheilagh, Vivienne, Doris, Linda, Zoe, Sue, Margaret, June, Jane, Elizabeth, Sue, Monica and Deanne. Also, to my dear wife and lovely daughter, my aunts, my two dear mums in this life, and all the other women and girls that have given of themselves for me. I extend my deepest thanks to Alison, Tammy, Hilary and Mary. Special thanks to Dr. R. and Mr. R. for opening the doors to my prison, and allowing me, at last, to live my life in the way it was always meant to be.

Thank you.

Joy

Chapter 1. Journey's End

Preparations were complete and an array of feminine items looked back at me from the shelf in the bathroom, challenging in their strangeness. It was June 23, 1989, a bright Thursday morning that saw me finalising the last details for the day's journey into the unknown.

Case packed and last cup of tea drunk, I had sat in the large living room where many hours of this new life had passed; the room was like a velvet capsule, where all my security and balance seemed concentrated. Hilary and Mary's 'goodbye for now' and 'see you soon' echoed in my ears, as the room began to rotate, and my whole being wanted to vomit. I felt like a condemned prisoner in his last moments, like a little boy who asks, '*Must* I go?' Had there been a way not to, I looked for it in those moments of abject fear. Sweat from my brow dripped onto my fresh, clean skirt, my legs trembled and I knew that if I stood up I would collapse from the weight of fear. As I tried to pull myself back from the brink, the whole of the past year flashed before me; all the pain and struggle sprang up, and the probability of defeat loomed large. I found my way to the bathroom and sat for several minutes on the lavatory in an effort to exorcise the feelings that roamed my body and mind. After some time, the horror passed and there came a cool peace and serenity, and I knew I was bound for my destiny, and that all the fear in my world was gone. I stood and looked at myself in the large bathroom mirror, blonde curly hair, blue eyes and a blue summer dress to match them. Around my neck hung the small gold locket with my only picture of my mother and one taken of my daughter when she was tiny, and beside the locket hung the tiny cross my dear friend Bill had given me especially for the coming event. Joy smiled back, calm now and confident in her new self, all apprehension dissolved away; this was what I had waited for and worried about for so long now - rebirth.

From then, the day ran smoothly. Mary drove me to the station, where I boarded the train to Brighton, and the small hotel room that was to entertain me for the next two days and serve as my womb. It was quiet there, the company of Mary's stuffed bear and my yellow knitted duck, smiling from the pillows on the bed, providing strange comfort.

The next day was one of silent hunger, my only sustenance being the black tea and Oxo drinks that I prepared frequently between the sachets of Picolax laxatives, the effects of which were without great discomfort. The day passed nicely enough, as I discovered the length of King's Parade, and found the Royal Pavilion. The two piers were like prehistoric monsters reaching out to sea, the one, broken now, looked like the other's mate, its rotting bones poking out of pea soup sea.

Saturday, and I rose at seven o'clock to spend a couple of hours on the sea front in the hot, early sunshine, drinking sweet black tea and watching men as they watched me with a hungry look, two of them making advances that at a future time may have made the mark. My real thoughts, though, were on the coming day, and the past seemed like the sea haze, indistinct, lost in history. Tomorrow, there would be a new me, doors to the future swinging wide to reveal pastures of peace and sunshine.

At nine forty-five, a short taxi ride from the hotel brought me to the last few steps I was to take as a man. There stood the clinic on the corner, quiet and private, its activities set apart from the world, awaiting the secret of my transformation. By ten thirty, I had been given yet another Picolax and two antibiotic tablets. My blood pressure and further blood samples were taken and I was left to sort out my new environment, placing the TV control and other essentials close to the bed, as I was to be confined to it for at least five days, my private parts trussed up in the tight bandages that were to support my new sex. The urologist who was to perform the operation told me he would 'sort me out in the morning'.

During the afternoon at the clinic I slept between the Picolax, and on waking there appeared, through the hazy orange of my closed eyelids, pictures of people's faces, soft and smiling. Maybe the two tablets taken earlier had been part of my pre-op; they certainly had a quieting effect on my mind.

At about three in the afternoon, there were more antibiotics and Picolax. I began to wonder if there would be anything left of my insides, and there was still an irrigation to come! At seven that evening, the young anaesthetist gave me three razors and asked if I would kindly shave my private parts in preparation for the morning. It was a sad sight to see *him* hanging there all pink and bald, but any sexual sensation had long gone, and he really had little use any more but to make my new vagina, the creation of which would complete my physical transformation.

I awoke to one of the noisiest dawn choruses ever! The sleeping pills taken the night before left me surprisingly clear thinking. It was five o'clock on my new birthday, June 25, 1989, the same date as my mother's birthday, and it had all the feeling of a full circle, as though perhaps some part of her might be reborn today, although hopefully not with the same enduring hardship she had suffered before her death on Easter Sunday, three years before. My stomach made loud rebellious noises as the last drops of fluid from yesterday's irrigation made their way to the sea. Nothing left now of the raspberry jelly and Oxo drinks; the irrigation procedure, whereby two feet of rubber pipe had been introduced into my bowel from the lower end, was certainly not painful, and nothing to fear. There was a feeling of inevitability, but it was so restful in the clinic that fear had long been removed. At some point before seven, the nurse came by and gave me three sleeping tablets in order to make me drowsy for the next few hours, and some twenty minutes later, through a haze, a voice told me he was going to put a needle in the back of my hand. I remember saying 'Huh Huh' and that was the last...

The room came slowly into view, and the sun was shining through the windows, onto me in my soft, cocoon-like bed. It was sometime during Sunday afternoon, the op was long gone, four hours of deep surgery had passed in perfect peace and the day was spent sliding in and out of sleep. There was no memory of what had gone before.

Monday was lousy. As the day tumbled its swaying, nauseous way through the long hours, the fact that there was something else between my legs was never far from my mind, and the gases that meandered their way through my insides became ever more desperate in their need for escape. At times, it became difficult to tell if they were in my bowel or in my bladder, which I understood to be attached to my new vagina. By the evening, all thoughts of food or comfort had completely vanished. There was now only the deep dull ache of massive surgery. Agony, followed by tears, filled my soul, and as the door of my room had been closed, there was, except for the silent tannoy, no contact with the world outside of this sea of pain and burning. Somewhere deep inside myself I could feel the length of my ex-penis on fire, and eventually, after some screaming of her name, the lovely Sandra came and administered the most relieving peace I had felt for the whole day. Once the comforting ice pack was between my legs, the opiate drug lowered me gently into sleep.

I woke very early the next morning, and the day passed between bouts of nausea and elation. At some point in the afternoon, the nurse came to change the whole dressing ensemble and remove the two drains that had been implanted. There was no pain, and for the first time I was able to see where my abdomen disappeared between my legs without the sight of that old familiar obstruction. I reflect on the whole thing as the most beautiful experience of my life. A magical feeling of warmth and security washed over me, and the nurses, with their special care and understanding, were all magicians.

Wednesday and Thursday passed in a nauseous millpond of dejection, and although the phone calls from Hilary and Mary were very welcome, they did not take away the feeling of utter loneliness. I looked longingly at the closed door and wished that some kind soul would open it and allow me some human contact. As the toxins in my stomach grew ever thicker, there seemed to be less and less room for the fresh drugs. I felt I was being poisoned from the inside, and when my loneliness turned to anger as I failed to grasp why I could not use the toilet to rid myself of the poisons, I found myself arguing with the nurses and lecturing them in physical logic and care of the human condition.

On the Friday afternoon, after what seemed an eternity, the urologist came, accompanied by two nurses, and removed the packing from my new vagina. Less obtrusive dressings were applied, and I was relatively free. I could now walk, though not without immense effort, and certainly not very far. As the days passed, the distances grew greater and my strength returned, and I was soon to be found all over the clinic. Still the catheter remained for a few days, a faithful but unwanted companion. Upon its stinging removal, I felt I had shed my ball and chain. Between the pack and catheter there were stitches to remove, each with a sharp bite, leaving behind very few outward signs that I had undergone gender reassignment and embarked on another life. The two longest stitches, some five inches long, stretched from my urethra at the top, almost to my anus underneath, one on either side, where the testes had been removed from the scrotum. Around the opening of the vagina there were some eight or ten smaller stitches, which formed the labial folds. The base of the penis disappeared somewhere inside me, and left the area looking as natural as nature ever intended. There is no clitoris, but where that bud should be, is the urethral opening, giving everything a very natural look. Of course, everything was swollen to three times its normal size, and the bruising spread for quite some distance all around the site, blue, orange and angry looking.

That Saturday, I was allowed my first bath, and sank thankfully into a very deep salt soak with my catheter hanging over the side. It was strange to see my new body for the first time, and I tried hard to remember how it had looked pre-surgery, but couldn't picture what had been between my legs before. It looked and felt natural, as though it had always been this way, and my childhood dream of being made into a girl had become a reality.

I had brought with me a large bottle of witch hazel, which, as soon as I was able to stand its coldness, I applied liberally day and night. Its effects were amazing, and within the first week most of the deep, more serious bruising was gone, leaving me able to sit in a more natural and comfortable position.

Then came the dilating. Some eight inches of solid Perspex in the shape of a cigar tube, inserted into the new vagina twice daily, after a salt bath, to maintain and stretch the inner walls. We, unlike genetic females, have no muscular walls to the vagina, so must exercise for ever the walls of our new sex, lack of dilation causing loss of penetrative depth. My progress went from strength to strength and the following Wednesday saw me winging my way back to Plymouth, with Hilary and Mary cocooning their precious cargo and taking special care to make the five-hour journey as comfortable as possible.

As I left the clinic, I looked at all the windows, and could plot every room. There was the bathroom, in which I had spent so many reflective hours, and on the floor below there were the new friends I had made in this place: charming, quiet women who accepted me as one of them, with all of the attendant problems. I was allowed into their world and felt honoured to be female. Somewhere in the heart of the clinic, was the theatre where Mr. R. had performed his magic upon me, completing the dream that had eluded and tormented me for so long. I reflected on that stone façade and wondered how many other silent façades held their secrets from the world.

Memories, yes, I have memories that will endure for ever, but there is no more pain, no more wondering why, just the peace of mind that came by way of the surgeon's knife.

Chapter 2. Early Years

My mother, Gladys, was one of three sisters, the other two being Ann and Marg. She was a highly strung, nervy woman, but appeared, on the surface, to enjoy life to the full, and was apparently 'one for the men'. Gladys married at the age of twenty-one, but met my father, who was from Hull, in the north of England, whilst her husband was on active service in the Navy, and on May 14, 1945, I was born in Plymouth, out of wedlock, a war baby and so called 'bastard' son of some other man.

Shortly after my birth, my mother's husband returned to the family home and my father left to collect his belongings from Hull, to settle in Plymouth. On his return, however, he found my mother living with her mother-in-law, her husband having moved in with a younger girl. My mother and father then set up home together and her husband cleared his belongings from the flat, shortly after which my mother found that she was pregnant by him. She gave birth to a little girl, Clare. Clare was soon taken into care, for adoption, as my mother was too ill to look after two young children, home life being punctuated by ever increasing visits to the local nerve clinic. One fateful day, she came home from the town to find my father in bed with the girl who lived in the flat above, a fight ensued and my mother was driven from the house, taking me with her to seek refuge at the home of her sister, my wonderful aunt Ann.

My mother's health deteriorated rapidly, and she was admitted to the local mental hospital some thirteen miles from the town, to be treated for severe depression. She was to spend the next sixteen years of her life there, losing almost all contact with the rest of her family, and me along with them. I was left in the care of my Aunt Ann, whilst my sister, who I never knew, was taken to Canada by a family, and never heard of again.

The photos of my mother showed her to be a slim, graceful woman with style, her bright, full face framed by a shock of curly brown hair. She had a quiet way of speaking and was extremely sensitive to the suffering of others. She absolutely adored animals, the weak and little ones taking a special place in her affections, and in later life she was never to be without a dog or cat, which I felt to be a substitute for the children she had so tragically lost to the state.

I lived with Aunt Ann until I was about four years old, happy years for me as I had the security I needed, in a proper family atmosphere. There were periods of upheaval, when I was farmed out to other aunts and uncles to give Aunt Ann a rest, as she also had two boys of her own to care for, but during these times, I would be allowed to visit her for tea on Sundays, and there was always a large jar of marmite in the middle of the table, bought especially for me, along with jelly, bread and butter and biscuits. In the early afternoons, with my aunt, I loved to bring in the food and lay it all out nicely on the table. Wonderful smells came from the kitchen when Ann cooked; I remember dinners, with the cabbage all piled up on the side, and the little plates on the dresser. All gleamed away in the soft light of the low powered bulb in the lamp speckled from flies that had settled there, the same as the specks covering the gilt-framed mirror over the mantelpiece at my mum's house. In the afternoon, there was the radio programme 'Sing Something Simple', and my aunt would drift off to sleep in the armchair, whilst my uncle would be out somewhere.

The eldest of my two cousins was Tony, a robustly built child with brown eyes and brown hair, who was strong and muscular and went on to become an army boxing champion. But my afternoons were spent colouring pictures or playing hide and seek in the tiny house with my favourite cousin, Billy. He was slender of body, clean, with lovely brown curly hair and brown eyes. He would sometimes read to me; there was no strain with him, no differences. When he got older, he bought a motorbike and let me sit on the seat while he wheeled it up and down the lane. Billy had a wonderful smile and I felt that his life had no deep problems, he was always so very happy. He was the closest male to me in the whole family. I suppose I loved Billy, in a way; he was different from all the other males, who seemed cold, distant and unfriendly. Billy was warm and protective towards me, as I always felt a man ought to be. He and I slept together in a double bed in a small room at the top of a narrow flight of stairs, at the back of the house. I can still feel his warm body, comforting, like a big bear. He had a lovely voice and would always let me choose which side of the bed I would like to sleep on. In the mornings, the sun would creep through the tightly drawn curtains like an orange mist.

Their father, my Uncle Tony, was a large set man with cropped hair, in the military style of the day. He had spent his whole national service in the Navy and had become very regimented.

He came from Yorkshire, and in my eyes was a most grumpy, complaining man who I avoided whenever possible. I knew he didn't like me; I was the unwanted bastard son of his wife's sister, and he consequently saw my mother as a slut. On occasions, there would be disagreements between my aunt and my uncle about me being there, and my aunt would cut him short in case I heard the exchange, which I often did. I grew to hate him, and on news of his death, years later, quietly cheered from somewhere deep inside that he was gone.

My Aunt Ann was a lovely, soft featured, quiet natured woman, not unlike my mother in looks, except that she had wavy black hair. She was slender of build and had a deep look in her eyes, not from sorrow, but more from a sense of inner calm. She seemed to extend the same soft love to me that my mother would have done had she been there. Perhaps she had all the things that most women were thought to want from life at her age - a relatively good husband, clean home and loving children. She seemed worry free, although she had not had an easy childhood herself, having spent some part of her life in an orphanage in the care of the local council. She was one of the loveliest women I had ever known; I suppose the love for her two other children had softened her. She loved me as her own, and at that time she was my only mother. I occasionally visited her, as did her own children, at the residential home where she spent the winter of her life, and it didn't come as a shock to her when I told her what I was going to do for myself; it was almost as if she expected it to happen, like she already knew.

My Aunt Marg was a small, delicately built, brown haired woman. Her features - narrow nose and small bright eyes - always reminded me of a little bird. Later in my youth, she showed a deep caring sincerity, as though she could take some of my loneliness away, but any love she had for me was watered down by the rather stiff, authoritarian, if not unfriendly attitude of my uncle Tim. He was a thin man who smoked a lot; he had ginger hair, a narrow face and long sinewy arms. I suppose he did attempt to play the father figure, but with no children of his own it didn't come easily.

My third aunt was called Edie, a healthy-looking woman with rosy skin and gingery blonde hair. She dutifully maintained a respectable distance between us, caring of my physical needs but nothing more. Uncle Henry, her husband, was of like mind, so I was tolerated out of a sense of duty to my mother. Their sons were likeable enough and I suppose we had some form of rapport, probably because we were thrown together, but I always felt as though I was different and on the fringes of their lives.

In retrospect, my three uncles were like a different species to me, and I found it difficult to relate to them. My aunties loomed large and importantly in my life and my uncles were strange, somewhat nefarious beings, who hovered at the edges of my world, living very private lives. From them came no instruction, no encouragement, nothing but cold indifference, and whilst my early childhood rolled away, I watched and learned what I could from my aunts.

In 1949, when I was four, the City Fathers decided enough was enough, and that if I wasn't placed very quickly in a permanent family environment, I would suffer serious damage and become extremely unstable. So it was that I started life in the deeply caring and all-encompassing love of my foster mother. Love poured from her like the heat from the sun on a hot summer day, she knew nothing else. In her lifetime, she had seen over fifty children go out into the world, all little orphan children like me, and was the most caring, loving and patient mother in the world. There was never an angry word, she loved every one of us as though we sprang from her own body. Her love knew no bounds, and she often went with little or no dinner to be sure we all had something. I wanted to be a 'good girl' for her, a feeling I had from the age of seven, having so strongly identified with my two sisters that I firmly believed myself to be just like them. To be just like them, I fetched the occasional bits of shopping and helped in the house with the cleaning, and watched closely as she did the ironing, cooking and mending of the socks, as though one day I might need to do the same for my own family.

'Mum' was about five foot six inches tall, quite stocky from years of heavy work, washing the clothes and bedding by hand, sweeping the house and making the beds. There was no man in the house to help her with the heavier work, because her husband had been killed whilst on the Lusitania, a passenger liner torpedoed during World War I. Her hair was straight and black, cropped in a straight line across the back of her neck, and the grey showed through at the sides, which were pinned back by a narrow hair slide. She had been born with a veiled left eye and had lost the eye in an attempt to remove the veil. I was always sensitive to this and often would not look directly at her face when she spoke to me, as it made me feel uncomfortable and sad for her. I loved her like no other. In the evenings we would sit and listen to 'Journey into Space', with Doc, Jet, Lemmy and Mitch, on the radio.

The room was lit by a gas light on the wall above the fireplace. It gave me the greatest pleasure to go to the shop at the top of the street and buy the delicate cotton mantle which came in its own little box and had a porcelain ring around the base, to stiffen it. To replace the broken one, I would climb up onto the mantelpiece, balance on my knees on that narrow ledge and very carefully twist the mantle onto the pins that held it in place. That done, it was time for the most exciting stage, which was to light the dome and watch the pure white cotton burn away to grey. To be trusted to hold a match, at that time, was something I positively strived for, as such dangerous things were not for small children. After the dome had burned away, I would very gently turn the tap at the side to let a jet of gas through. As I turned the gas up, the room filled with soft, clear light. It was almost fairy-like, and Mum kept this little operation just for me!

In winter, below this mantelpiece, there was a lovely fire, which I was allowed to help build. First the newspaper, then a pyramid of thin sticks of wood that came tied together with a thin strand of wire. Sometimes it was a real struggle to get the twist of wire undone, upon which the sticks would spill into the grate, giving out a musical sound as they struck the hearth on their ends. In the mornings, we would sift through the grey powdery ash to find the unburned embers, to keep them to start the next fire. The grate and hearth were dense black in colour, regularly polished with Zebo, grate polish of the time. It was lovely to see the shine, as the dirt from the previous evenings fire was brushed away, revealing the metal below. At the side stood the fire irons, with gleaming brass handles and long iron blades.

Doreen was the youngest female living at the house during my time there. She was the same age as I was, a pleasantly made girl with reddish ginger hair and freckles and a slight speech impediment. We were sisters - that's how it seemed, anyhow. There were no boy's clothes in the house, so for the first year I wore dresses and knew no different. We played at nurses, and mummies and babies, and took turns to take the dollies for a walk in the pram that lived under the stairs, where every other interesting thing ended up. There was never any strife between us; we worked perfectly together.

Then there was my eldest sister, Jane. She was much older than me, with a mystery about her that made her special. There is no doubt in my mind that I was deeply in love with my sister Jane, and this was a love that was to last for the rest of my life. She was slender, with a beautifully balanced face, framed with light brown hair to the nape of her neck. She radiated calmness and equanimity with every movement, and I could tell from her body scent when she had been in the room. Somewhere inside me, Jane had her own special niche. I suppose I identified with her in a way beyond my limited comprehension. She taught me to knit, and I would sit and sew things and crochet and make small round doilies. In my young mind, had it been possible, I would have married her. I would often watch her make up before she went out in the evenings to meet her boyfriend, Bill, who she met at Leggo-Wilson laundry, where she worked, and who later became her husband. Bill and I were like oil and water, we never mixed. Maybe he sensed my possessiveness. I learnt an awful lot from watching Jane, as though I was in some form of apprentice-ship. Subconsciously, I was fascinated by the way she coloured her lips and rolled the tissue between them to remove the excess lipstick; her effect on me went deep.

Then there was my elder brother, Mike, a slinky kind of man who I never saw much of, but used to hear shout at Mum that he had no shirt to wear, and tell her she should iron one now! He was about eighteen years old and spent most of his nights in coffee bars and gambling places in the town, most times coming home in the early hours of the morning. He was very proud of his Teddy Boy drape coats and thick soled shoes, all perfect. He seemed to have an ordered life from where I stood, but our paths rarely crossed. Sometimes, I would find his girlie mags under his mattress; I loved to see the naked girls and fantasise that I looked like them, wishing that I too could have breasts and a lovely face and long hair. Mike's was one room in the house that I saw very rarely. Like Mum's front room, it was sacrosanct, and no one was allowed there.

On bath nights, Mum would bring the tin bath from the back yard to the kitchen, and boil lots of kettles of water. My sister Doreen and I would take turns at being the first one in the bath, whilst the other would sit on the Rexine covered box seats that made part of the fire fender and held the coal. The fire, mixed with the light from the gas light on the wall, threw dancing shadows around the room, reflected in the big mirror at the centre of the mantelpiece. This room was the heart of the house; everything happened here: games and reading, colouring and puzzles, dollies and beds for them all. It was dimly lit and had more character than rooms of today.

I had to be taken up the stairs by Mum, or Jane when she was there, because there was a big landing window, and for several months I thought I could see a horrible face looking in from the yard outside, perhaps the face of an ape. One day, whilst I was in the toilet in the yard, with the door closed, there appeared the biggest spider that I had ever seen in my life. I screamed out in fear, and Mum's son, Uncle Steve, who was home from sea, came out of the house and killed it for me. I was afraid of that toilet for a long time afterwards and would want to use the potty in the house. Then I would get my legs smacked for sitting instead of standing at it for my wee, which was all I had ever seen my sister Doreen do and to me was the natural way. Mum expressed her concern to Uncle Steve on more than one occasion, about my girl-like behaviour, and I would scream the house down when she tried to take away my pram and dollies. Uncle Steve would come to my rescue and tell Mum that I would grow out of it.

Our food was quite plain but wholesome and nourishing. On Sundays, there was often breast of lamb with roast potatoes and cabbage cooked in soda, with white bread and margarine, never butter. Christmas was a time of parties put on by the Navy, on the HMS Eagle or the Ark Royal. They were fantastic ships, like cities; we never got to see all of the ship, there seemed to be hundreds of passageways and hatchways, with thick steel doors, and there was always a smell about these places that one never smelled elsewhere. It was the peculiar smell of paint and metal and life spent in a metal container.

Sometimes, we would go to one of the orphanages and gather round a large Christmas tree to collect presents sent in by people living in the town. They lay waiting for us, with our names written on brightly coloured labels. There was a Father Christmas, who asked in traditional manner what our names were and gave us the presents. There were always lots of sweets to take home with us in the evening, a lasting reminder, for some days, of the party, with the special sweet kept to the very last. I would see all the little girls in their best frocks and dresses and wish I could look as pretty as them. I pulled the bits of fluff from the front of my grey school pullover, which had been freshly washed for the occasion and matched the grey short-legged trousers I wore with it. They were an exact replica of the clothing I wore to school each day, but were kept for best. Short grey socks and brown shoes completed the outfit, which was comfortable and clean, nothing more.

At home we always had chicken for Christmas dinner; turkey was for the rich people at the far end of town where they had lots of money. I enjoyed watching Mum pluck the feathers from the bird. There was always a great pile of sticky feathers, some of which swirled to the floor and blew about from the draught that came under the back kitchen door. When the feathers were off, she would proceed to take out the insides; her hands were large and strong, decorated by a single gold wedding band which gleamed dull yellow amongst the sticky contents of the bird. I could barely watch her when she did this, but was intrigued to see how many eggs there were inside, without shells. Sometimes as many as six eggs would appear on the table amongst the multi-coloured pile of guts and organs that had been taken from the bird, and then the neck would join them. Mum was a cook of the old school.

At lighting up time, the lamplighter would come to the lane beyond the high wall at the back of the house. The streetlights were gas fired and he would push a long stick into the underside of the lamp post and turn on the gas, which made a clinking sound, then he would light the lamp. Later, they replaced the gas lamp with an electric one, and the gas lighter was no more to be seen; the rag and bone man suffered the same fate, so gone were the few pennies that would be our reward for the worn out woollens that we had to give. I can remember going to the grocery shop with the ration card, for sugar, tea, etc. In the evenings there were very often udder sandwiches. The Polish butcher two streets away used to pick the best of it for us; it was a soft pink colour, sweet tasting, with the texture of luncheon meat. I loved it! Just as well, for we ate enough of it. I can remember the butcher at the top of our street saying, 'I've got a present for you, hold out your hand.' I did, and he handed me a pig's brain - it was revolting, I never went there again. That summer, there was a tremendous thunderstorm, and a fire ball went through his top bedroom window, destroying the room entirely. You could hear the bang from streets away; perhaps that was his reward for his trick with the brain.

Chapter 3. School Days

I was happy enough. I was fed and watered and eventually started school in the infants at Prince Rock School. It was the large school for boys, some few streets away from my house, which had originally been an approved school and was reputed to be the hardest around. Some quarter of a mile away, on the side of a steep hill, stood the Salisbury Road School, for girls. I often wondered why I couldn't go to that school instead, trying to project myself into its mysterious interior and imagine myself at the desk amongst all the other girls. Sometimes, if I stayed away from school for the day, I would listen to the shrieks of fun and laughter that came from their playground.

At the boys' school, I didn't relate to the rough games and noisy shouting. The boys were particularly rough in their manner of speech, and very often there were fights. Often, I would close my hands over my ears to shut out the din. I was afraid of the violence and would keep well out of the way when it erupted incase I became involved.

I found an advert in the papers for a Charles Atlas body building course and spent several months trying to improve the appearance of my puny body to make it more muscular and attractive. I gained strength, but not the confidence to use it in my defence. On my way home from school, I would see all the girls in their black skirts and blue blouses, and they always held a fascination for me. They were of my kind, and yet I was separated from them. They were different, gentler in their ways and quieter talking than the boys with whom I now had so much contact. There seemed to be a stronger bond and deeper feeling between the girls than there was between the boys, who were always on some kind of adventure, always active, excited and noisy. The girls moved more slowly, and I suppose it reminded me of the way nuns walked, quietly and gently. The seeds of motherhood moved in their bodies and I could sense the softness of their being, whilst the boys seemed hard and aggressive, fast moving and threatening. They enjoyed the excitement of the chase, and it was as if inflicting pain brought them some kind of perverted pleasure. It seemed then, as now sometimes, that the world wasn't a safe place to be on your own, the human jungle snatching and grabbing at you from every rock and tree, particularly by the male of the species. No, I didn't enjoy their company - unless they showed some kind of love towards me, in which case I was lost to my feelings.

One memory of Prince Rock school is of the science master who had fought in the First World War and been injured by mustard gas. I was possibly the only person to feel sad for him. I also remember crates of milk in little glass bottles, at break time, which I drank as much of as I possibly could, because milk was not normally available at home. Woodwork was a complete mystery to me, and I positively hated metalwork, with its cold, hard sharpness, and the discomfort of horrible gritty steel between my fingertips. I didn't mix with the rest of the boys very much, and had only one or two close friends. I spent most of my day alone in my own little world, where I would fantasise about other countries and exotically named places. Sometimes, I would spend ages walking home after school, daydreaming about all sorts of obscure things, such as where all the little birds slept at night. I would look at the girls and wonder why they were different, why I wasn't like them and why I couldn't play with them in the park, where they shooed me away like they would all the other boys. I felt ostracised and didn't know why. I was not a boy, I was my sister's sister, and I thought that they would somehow sense it and let me join in. On the rare occasions I was allowed, they would keep me on the fringes of their games, standing there in those short grey trousers, feeling stupid and at a total loss. But I still enjoyed the little that I got from them, and then it was like the times Doreen and I played together.

I didn't learn much at school, and was always at the bottom of the class for most subjects, except Art and English, the rest was just a mess. In junior school I came a regular thirty-fourth place in a class of thirty-four, a position usually shared with my best friend. We were put at the back of the classroom where we could see nothing and thereby consolidated our position as the class idiots. Although I did very well at sport, I hated football, and the first experience of this game put me off for life. We were on a huge football pitch of dried mud, and I felt my thin little ankles might snap at every step on the stone hard, broken earth, I was always of delicate build - a skinny little waif. We were led into a dirty hut at the edge of the field, with benches all around the walls. The floor was covered with dried earth from previous games, and the whole place was filthy dirty. I was presented with a pair of boots large enough for two of us to get into, and a pair of shorts which hung to my calves, also big enough for two of us. On the field of play there was bedlam as the other boys ran hither and thither after a large dirty ball which, when it hit me, felt as hard as stone and rough on my skin. It was an awful experience and I just stood in one spot for the whole of the game, not knowing what to do or where to go. It was the first and last time I ever went onto a football pitch, and the vision of those boots, with their sticky surface and the strange looking studs on the bottom, some missing, of course, remained with me.

It was on the edge of that field that I learned to ride a bike. There were no bikes in the street where I lived. This one was brand new and belonged to my friend who lived a few houses away from me, the only other boy in the street. His family were quite well off and he was the only one that I knew to have a new bike. I fell off it the first time and thought I had broken it; he looked ever so worried, because his mother had forbidden anyone else to ride it. It wasn't a small bike, and to ride it I had to stand on the pedals, there was no way I could reach the seat. As my lessons progressed, my confidence increased and soon I was able to ride quite a long way, but I wished they had not put that silly cross bar in the way.

On some afternoons, when his mum was in the town after school, my friend and I would play with each other; his penis was as big as a man's and his ejaculation was copious to say the least, whereas mine was virtually non-existent. There was no harm in what we did at the time, but unknown to me I was adding to the many problems that beset my life; most boys grew out of that stage, I never did.

At the top of the street there lived a girl who had a terrible reputation with the boys. It never interested me to find out what she did with them; the very idea of being near her frightened the life out of me. It was almost as though I thought she would eat me, so I avoided her whenever possible. She was the only one who could swing right over the bar in the park, and one day she went over the bar but was not fast enough to stop herself from falling from the top, hitting the concrete floor and breaking a few bones. No one ever tried again.

Chapter 4. Discoveries

My first sexual experience with a girl was on a sunny afternoon with my friend and his cousin. He lay on her and did something I couldn't see, then got up and told me it was my turn. I lay on her and rubbed my limp penis against her body, but there was absolutely none of the sensation I had heard about. I was about ten years old, and my dinner was more important to me than some elusive pleasure, so I went home to my dinner and he went home with his cousin.

Time after time, I got caught stealing, and was eventually expelled from Princes Rock, taken into the care of an orphanage and sent to a new school, mixed this time and much more agreeable to me. In the first, and as it happened, last term in this school, I reached the position of second in the class in some subjects, and not lower than fourth or fifth for any. They were the best results I was ever to attain in any school, art being my best subject. The first few weeks were fine, but I got bored with the same bowl of flowers, and wanted to go upstairs to the life class, where girls were sitting naked for everyone to draw. I would have gladly sat there with them and shown off my beautiful body, had I had one; the body I had never seemed very special to me.

Instead, I wandered into the dressmaking class. I was perfectly at home there, in tune with the girls and as comfortable in their presence as I once was with Doreen, but eventually my art teacher found me. He hit the roof, as he had searched for six weeks, that being the last place he expected to find me. I retired from the school pretty quickly after that.

I spent most of my spare time at the railway sidings, where grass grew long and thick, and there was an air-raid shelter under the ground. The older boys would take girls there; the old paper brought for them to lie on was left to get damp, and the whole place stank. One day, I dragged an old Christmas tree in there and got on the wrong side of it as I set it on fire. It was as dry as tinder, and in a second the narrow tunnel was full of black, acrid smoke, so thick that I couldn't see the entrance and had to lie on the filthy floor to escape. I was in a dreadful state - thank goodness for Persil. Another time, we built a fire in the middle of the grass and on this fire was a piece of old lino that caught alight at the corner. I picked up the opposite end and chased my friend with it, but as I ran, the grass behind me caught fire. Within minutes, the flames were twenty feet high, with the breeze fanning them up the siding. The Fire Brigade arrived with two engines. It was time to go home!

On sunny weekends I would go to a high hill outside of town, to be alone and look over the water and the countryside. It was quiet there; the butterflies sometimes landed on my sleeve and if I was very still and quiet the birds would come up close. I buried the little bodies of my pets up there, each in a jar of vinegar, hoping it would eat away the flesh and leave the bones clean, so that when I retrieved them later I could reconstruct the skeletons to form a collection of specimens. I don't know if it worked; I suppose those jars must still be there to this day. It was a lovely place to study nature undisturbed, looking right out over Saltram Park and the river Plym. Below me was the place where they broke ships for scrap, and there was the slaughterhouse and glue makers, which smelled disgusting. Sometimes I would see train loads of bones being brought in for processing.

Although there were beaches, they were too far away to reach without a car or bus, and in those days there were very few cars and no money to pay a bus fare, even though it amounted to only a few pennies - the big copper ones, with Britannia on one side. I used to look forward to pocket money day, and the amount I was given increased as I grew older. I started with sixpence per week, rising to two shillings, and at the orphanage I got five shillings. The greatest prize was to get it in the form of two half-crowns, big heavy coins that I didn't want to spend because they were so beautiful! Sixpences were lovely, small and silver in colour, sometimes I would get a real silver one, but most times it was an ordinary sixpenny bit. The farthings were pretty too, with a little wren on the back, four to every penny. Sweets were ever so cheap, and you could get a bag of chips for threepence. One day I found a five-pound note in the street and went screaming with excitement the whole way home. A woman stopped me and said it was hers, but I just ran on, the only thought in my mind being to give it to my mum. I was so proud at having found it, I got some new clothes, and we had a few special things: a big colouring book, some models to make, and even a trip to the pictures. The small things were very special in those days - it was all anyone had.

As a youth, I was very interested in gynaecology and by the age of eight or nine knew the technical terms for the female sex organs, from some old midwifery books, although I had no information about the sex act itself. Some years later, I discovered a book called Cochinell, about a French boy who had a sex change. I think it must have been one of the first recorded cases. It described the operation in detail, and I stored this description in my mind, alongside other medical information. Surgery held a curious fascination for me at that time, and over the years, has helped me understand how my own body works. At the time they were just interesting facts that one did not ordinarily hear about, but the contents of these books were to have serious implications that followed me through my life. The book, Cochinell, described how they took out the inside of this boy's penis and made a vagina with the skin; I don't remember what the book said about the pain and trauma he must have suffered, it is so long ago, but there was no turning back from that time. Although it took many years to manifest itself, I was completely fascinated by the idea that I too would one day be made into a girl, and I would often pull my penis down between my legs and make it all smooth there. I felt that girls were made, and it didn't occur to me that there could be two distinct sexes from birth. Patiently I waited to be changed into the little girl that I felt myself to be, although in later years, the bulge between my legs prevented me from wearing revealing female clothing and denied me the feeling of being complete.

My room was the biggest, on the first floor, at the front of the house. It spanned the passageway below and was my domain. It had two large windows on the front wall, the chimney wall had cupboards on either side, and on the wall opposite the windows was my bed. It was a double bed, but I never shared it with anyone. The room behind mine was where my sister Doreen slept. It was big enough for a single bed and chest of drawers. One night, I went to her room, lifted back the covers and stood there looking at her nakedness. I just didn't understand why there was a difference, why, although we were the same, and sisters, we were so different down there. Suddenly, my elder sister Jane appeared from nowhere and I got a healthy hiding for being there. Sometime later, Doreen was taken from the house to live with another family and I lost the only friend I had in the home. Looking back, I suppose they were only thinking of her safety. The Children's Department replaced her with a boy, James, who was to take her room and her bed, but not her place.

I hated James on sight. The space in my world had shrunk, no more was it exclusively ours, there was a cuckoo in the nest, and I resented it deeply. I wasn't used to boys at home at all, only at school, and now, here was James. He was horrible: tall like a skeleton with skin on, with hardly any hair at all on his head, and the hair he had was almost colourless. His skin was so thin that his veins showed through, blue. He was horrible and he was there to stay. I never lost my hate for him, and on many a morning I would hit him as hard as possible in the face to ensure that I left him hanging over the sink in the kitchen bleeding profusely from the nose. One night, I caught him sleeping on his back with his mouth open. I hated to see him there in my sister's bed, and I peed straight into his open mouth, hoping he would drown or choke to death. In retrospect, I believe I was hurting the mirror image of myself, a self which I hated and in no way resembled that of my now missing sister, she the like of which I felt myself to be. He was mine to terrorise as I wished, and terrorise him I did, with no mercy; I hated him, but never knew why.

We had a cat, a dear, thirteen-year-old whisky cat that had been there since before I arrived. We were great friends. At night, it would sleep on the rug in front of the fireplace. One morning, we came down to find it had died in its sleep, just where it lay. We also had a large ex police dog called Kim. I would often ride on its back. One day, Kim stole a broom from the school, but no one came to claim it from us! Uncle Steve had got the dog for us. I always had the deepest regard for him; he was my favourite uncle of them all. He was in the Merchant Navy and would bring back presents from places like Hong Kong and Australia. Mum put them all in the front room, where the curtains were always drawn, and no one ever went. I think she kept it sacred to the memory of her husband. One time, Uncle Steve brought me a bar of Toblerone chocolate in a triangular box, a luxury in those days, looking as strange as it tasted; I didn't like it at all! He also brought a lovely lacquered box with drawers and doors, for Mum. After her death, the little box became mine but was always left with my sister Jane for safe keeping. I guess it's still there to this day.

In the back yard, I kept my menagerie, mainly pigeons, along with a baby sparrow that I found injured in the street. The sparrow lived in a cage with two pigeons, one of which would try to shake it about, but the other would take it under its wing and protect it, which was very touching to watch. I felt that the aggressive one would never get to hurt the sparrow. We would often go to the park together and I would let it forage around in the fresh green grass, I loved that little bird and it seemed to know, from the way it looked back at me directly with its small brown trusting eyes. It was a beautiful, helpless little thing, a victim in life, and mine to love and care for. I also kept a newt or two and dozens of tadpoles in the spring. One of the newts died so I took it into the street on the front wall and opened its body with a safety razor that I kept for my craft work, but as soon as its insides came into view I passed out cold. There was a horrible singing in my ears and a spinning sensation. The next thing I knew I was waking up on the pavement: I never did any more autopsies.

In the summertime, it was lovely to go to the park to play, and to build houses from the piles of fresh mowed grass from the motor mower that the man rode about on, round and round, the sweet smell of the grass mixed with the occasional whiff of exhaust fumes. I could hear the click of bowls on the green, where the older men spent their long summer afternoons, and watching them walking up and down in their soft white shoes, flat white hats and jackets, would wonder what the game was all about.

One year, we had a particularly bad bonfire session. A roman candle firework that someone had thrown, went down my friend's wellington boot. His injuries were terrible. He had to have plastic surgery all the way up the right-hand side of his body where the fireballs from the thing had flared up at him from their vantage point in his boot, there being no way he could get it out till it had spent itself. On the day after bonfire night, on the way to school, armed with matches, I collected the carcases of the fireworks that lay about the place. I carefully removed their insides, put them into a small bottle and rested it on the front wall of a house; I wanted to know whether the flame from a match would die of oxygen starvation before the powder ignited. There was a tremendous flash of light and a searing pain in my eyes. I had blinded myself. I ran screaming down the street and was taken to a house from where the ambulance took me to the eye infirmary. I could feel the brushes that they used to clean my eyeballs, but saw nothing. I lay in the ward for six weeks, in total darkness. The headmaster from the school, who instilled fear in his pupils, ruled with an iron hand, and later expelled me with 'six of the best', came to visit me, bringing a large bottle of orange juice, the kind you dilute. I was surprised at the human warmth he was able to find on the occasion of my hospitalisation. During my stay in the hospital, all my little animals went. The little sparrow that had so often accompanied me to the park was taken to Torquay to live with my Aunt Bernice, Jane's real mother. It was a very sad homecoming, to all those empty cages.

My foster mother's strength diminished and her health grew gradually worse. One wash day, I was in the house alone with her. In the corner of the kitchen stood the ubiquitous copper boiler, going full tilt, with steam puffing from the edges of the lid and the gas burner beneath it showing blue flames. There was a space of about eighteen inches between that and the gas oven, roasting hot with the dinner inside. Mum stood in front of the cooker, facing it, then slowly fell forwards into the space between cooker and boiler, completely unconscious. I grabbed her sleeve to pull her from the gap, but she was firmly wedged between the two roasting machines. I ran, screaming, to the top of the street, where my sister Jane had set up home, and was lucky to find her there. After that, life was a swirl of activity: we weren't allowed to see our mum, cases were packed and we were bundled off to the local orphanage, Astor Hall.

Chapter 5. Lost and Found

Here was an experience which opened my eyes to a new, noisy world. Dozens of children ran everywhere, and toys were either shared or snatched away, disappearing into the depths of the huge playroom. Astor Hall, named after Lady Astor, was a mansion in its own grounds, massive compared to the tiny little house I had come from. It had a park all to itself, with large trees; today it is run as a care home. My first taste of this place came within half an hour of being there. We were in this large playroom and I was with some strange woman from the welfare, when a gangly, pale, skeleton-like woman came over to us, who could have been James' mother. I had brought a toy of some sort, and held it in my arms. She snatched this toy from me and passed it to one of the other children, who promptly disappeared with it. The fire rose up in me, and I screamed as loud as I had ever screamed; I was wild. Her action and my reaction ensured that we were to become mortal enemies for the whole length of my stay there. One evening, we were sitting at the dinner table, a very long wooden affair, with children along both sides of it.

First there were prayers - something unheard of in my childhood but I mumbled along with the rest. Then came dinner, fried liver - I had never seen liver in my entire life and had no idea what it was. I very gingerly ate round this dark substance on my plate; no words can describe what it looked like to me, and eventually it was the only thing left. I cut a small piece from the corner of the substance and put it in my mouth, it was absolutely disgusting. What was this horrible thing? It tasted like nothing on earth. I deposited it on the side of my plate directly from my mouth, without spitting; it was perfectly dry, and there was no way that I was going to allow it down my throat. Then the ogre was behind me! Skeleton woman had discovered me and my uneaten liver.

'What's this, then?' she demanded.

'I don't like it, Miss!' I replied.

'You will eat all of your dinner,' she said, as my head was tugged back by the hair and the liver was forced in great lumps into my mouth. There was no escape, she had me well and truly pinned against the back of the chair, and in it went, all of it, and down it went too, until the plate was cleared. But this little fiasco was short lived and her moment of glory quickly over, for no sooner had she released me from her grip, than my stomach took over the proceedings and shot the lot right down the middle of the table; sick and chewed liver everywhere. She sent me to bed early that evening, without supper.

One afternoon, as we walked back from school, two by two, my brother James was in front of me. To see him there brought my old hate for him to the surface, and I started to rile him up. For the first time ever, he retaliated; he spun round and the next minute we were both on the pavement, fighting like a couple of snakes. It was then that, lo and behold, I saw skeleton woman's skinny form through the legs of excited children. Trapped by the children all around her, she had no escape from my flailing feet, and paid for all her injustices towards me with the tremendous kicking I proceeded to inflict. James was completely forgotten about, as he was never any competition anyway. After that, skeleton woman avoided me like the plague.

We spent three months in that unhappy place before we saw our mum again. On her return she looked extremely unwell and tired; it had taken an awful lot out of her and she was never to recover her original strength and energy. She wore a massive plaster cast around her body and I later learned that she had a slipped disc. Her robust form didn't help the situation. James was moved to another home, which just left Mike and me. Gone were the days when Mum and I would walk the two miles needed to visit her sister, who had the only television for miles around. Her front room would be full of viewers from the neighbouring flats, all crowded round that twelve inch screen. I saw the coronation of Elizabeth II at her house, and I will never forget the serial of Quatermass and the Pit, which was absolutely terrifying. Mum and I would walk all the way home in the dark, clutching each other for protection, a ridiculous situation as I was too small to protect her, and she was too old to protect me. I remember the day they came to remove the cast from around her body; it was large enough for me to sit inside, like a roofless igloo, and as ungainly as Uncle Pip's greatcoat from the First World War, which lay in the hallway cupboard and was too massive and heavy for me to lift.

I would go to see Uncle Pip, Mum's long-standing darling, on Sunday mornings, for breakfast. He was a huge man from County Cork and had seen action in France, during the First World War. He was a one-time member of the Black Watch, and had lots of medals, including the honour of the Croix De Guerre. He would always ask me 'how many eggs?' and I would say 'the same as you, Uncle Pip.' We would have two, or even three, boiled eggs each. He smoked a pipe and would cut the tobacco up and shred it finely with his old penknife, then rub it in the palm of his hand. Sometimes, I did this for him, before stuffing it into the bowl of his pipe, and he would light it up till thin curls of smoke issued from the bowl. Then he would sit smoking, in a wet sucking way, often having to light the pipe again. One day, I asked if I could have a go on his pipe. I sucked the smoke back into my lungs as I had seen my sister do when she smoked her cigarettes. The room went a distinct green colour as I fell back on the bed, and I stayed there for the rest of the afternoon, positively ill, feeling as if I had been poisoned.

Things weren't all normal with Uncle Pip. Sometimes he would sit on the edge of the bed, pull me gently to him and fondle my genitals. As I had never been taught right from wrong, I let him continue, I had had no sex education up until then, so never knew to say no; I was fed, watered, loved, and nothing more. At that time, sex was a dirty word, never mentioned except in the most private of company, and then only between adults, never in front of the children. The subject was undercover, as would be a divorce, or some illicit, adulterous affair between married people. Uncle Pip never hurt me physically and I never questioned what he did, it never dawned on me to complain to anyone. Sometime later, my cousin got me some work in a fish and chip shop, peeling the potatoes in a machine, then putting them in the chipper so they spewed forth as chips into the bucket below. My boss at the chip shop also abused me and often as not I would masturbate him into a tissue. I was always paid extra for this and never felt any guilt.

Uncle Pip moved to a more modern flat in the centre of town, on the first floor, at the top of a flight of concrete steps. He suffered with shrapnel wounds received in the war, the pieces left in, rather than removed. The wounds wept continuously and there was always an oddly sweet smell in his room, somewhat akin to mushrooms. One day, he fell down the stairs and cracked his hip; he never recovered from this fall and died shortly afterwards. Mum was heartbroken.

Shortly after Mum's return from the hospital, I was taken away to a children's home and was only able to visit her when they allowed it. On Sundays, I would run away to see her, and the police would come to her house and collect me, as they always knew where I was. On one such visit, a few months after Uncle Pip's death, I came into the street where she lived and was singing in my head 'Come on and hear, come on and hear Alexander's Ragtime Band,' to myself. It was a lovely day, and the sun shone overhead. Everything was quiet, as Sundays are. When I got to the house, my sister, Jane, took me aside and told me that Mum had died of a heart attack in the night. My brother, Mike, had found her. There was no pain. The news went in and stayed there. I didn't feel sad enough to cry, and didn't know whether or not I ought to. I somehow felt I needed permission; it seems my conditioning was thorough and deep. I had seen death on lots of occasions with my little animals, it was no stranger. I was not, of course, allowed to be at the funeral, another adult secret that I didn't understand, just like all the rest.

Before being taken away to the children's home, I had a sweetheart who was beautiful in my eyes. Susan and I were madly in love with each other, and I would try my best to comfort her on lonely evenings when her mother drank herself into oblivion. I visited her mother in the hospital when she slid into an alcoholic stupor, which eventually killed her. It was awful to see her, like a thin grey rabbit, cheeks sunken and eyes forming deep sockets in her head, where lived death. I only went to see her once, she died soon afterwards. I suppose, in a way, Susan reflected my own loneliness and was also the replacement I needed for my sister, Doreen, as someone I could trust and relate to.

I was no angel as a child and often cried myself to sleep at the things I had said in defiance, to Mum. Once, I said I wished she was dead, but I think it was probably my own death that I wished for, as I already hated myself. After she died, I could feel her watching me from somewhere out there. I had been brought up as a Salvationist, so at least had some religious education. I used to go to Sunday school, but most times I would only be there long enough to get the blue star stamped in my attendance book, before going off to the Hoe, or up to my favourite hill on the other side of town. I could never really believe what they taught me about God and the angels, but I used to love the Sermon on the Mount, and it kept my soul together at times when I was on the road many years later. I always felt that somewhere, the maker of all things was watching over me and would never let any real harm come to me, even in the darkest of moments. Later, I was to find out how dark those moments could be, when all the demons in Hell hounded me into a whirlpool of mental pain and inner suffering.

One year, I was one of the Three Kings in the Nativity play. The stage had different levels, like wide steps, the robes I wore were long and cumbersome, and I fell down the steps in front of a hall full of spectators. I felt foolish, my sense of inferiority growing stronger with each stupid act, and I retreated into my shell, viewing the world from a fortress I constructed around myself, which served to protect my soft inner feelings. My introversion grew deeper as the years rolled by, until emotional communication with others became almost impossible and I viewed everyone with suspicion. It seemed I was to spend the rest of my life searching in strange places to find my identity, a self I occasionally glimpsed but didn't know how to reach and materialise, so kept locked away from the world. I remembered Jesus' words: '...neither cast ye your pearls before swine, lest they trample them under their feet, and turn again to rend you.' So my treasured image of myself remained a deep secret.

In 1958, when I was thirteen, a woman from the Children's Department took me to a hospital and told me I was to meet my mother. As far as I was concerned, Mum was dead, so who was this other woman that was being called my mother? The hospital was a maze of shiny yellow painted walls and corridors, lit with a light diffused by frosted glass windowpanes. There were strange people who walked about and talked to themselves, and said things to me that I didn't understand. There was no apparent way out of the building once you were in there; I can remember thinking how easy it would be to get lost in it all. I sometimes heard screaming and shouting coming from a long way away, in some other part of the hospital, and I was totally bewildered by the place. I was introduced to a woman, sitting on a bench in the garden, and we were left to talk to each other. I didn't know her at all; she could have been anyone, except for the affection in her eyes as she looked long at me with a soft smile on her face. A deep sense of loss and love radiated from her, and she projected warmth towards me, so I sat on the bench with her and we talked. She asked me what hobbies I had and I told her, then I mentioned I was a patrol leader in the Scouts. She rolled back her sleeves and showed me the scars on her wrists that she'd got from smashing a window. She pointed to the veins and said, 'They're Scouts, too.'

My stomach turned and I became suddenly very frightened of her. I wanted to back away and glanced anxiously about the surrounding garden to ascertain whether there was anyone else that I could draw comfort from. The meeting between us now had a sinister feeling about it, a feeling of foreboding, and instilled in me a fear of mental illness. I never went to see her again in the hospital and lived my life in dread of ending up in the same place as her. I thought madness was hereditary, which frightened me, and led me, in my darkest hours, to question my sanity.

During 1959, I met my father. He was a big man - about six feet tall with a shock of ginger hair that cascaded to his shoulders. His face was buried in a large red beard; he was, to say the least, formidable looking, the proprietor of a second-hand shop in Plymouth's famous Union Street. His home, on the first floor of the building, consisted of two rooms and a kitchenette. The sitting room was unforgettable, I had never seen anything like it before. There was one window that looked out on to the back of the building behind the house, and there was no other view. The wall next to the window wall had a painting on it that went from skirting to picture rail and stretched along the full length of the room. It depicted the view from Mount Edgcumbe to the Hoe. The wall facing the window was similarly painted, but the scene was from the Hoe to Cattedown. The third clear wall, all bar the door, had on it the view from Cattedown to Mount Batten. The complete scene covered the room; he had painted the lot from memory, as his piece-de-resistance.

I had learned from my aunt that he was called Jack, and upon our first meeting, I innocently called him Jack. 'You call me Dad, not Jack,' was his answer from some great height. That day, he gave me the first watch I had ever owned. It was a Kienzle self-winding watch, a heavy thing with a weight that swung around inside to wind it. I wore it in the bath because it said 'waterproof' on the back; needless to say, it never went again, and I was afraid to tell him. His booming voice stayed in my memory, and I saw him as a giant, like the giant of Jack and the Beanstalk fame. On this first visit, he also asked me if I would like to go to Australia with him, but I said I would stay in England with my mother, who was still in the hospital at that time. I don't know why I suddenly showed allegiance to a woman I hardly knew, unless it came from fear of the absolute unknown that presented itself in the shape of my father. Perhaps it was an instinctive way of protecting myself against him, or perhaps I felt he was like my many uncles and I closed my inner doors against him. On my second visit to his shop he was gone, and there was a sign on the door: 'Gone to Australia'. Below it was an address, but I had nothing to write with, and the next time I went there, it too had gone. My efforts to find him have failed, but I have often felt as if I would like to kill him for the way he treated my mother.

Chapter 6. Misfit

It was my last few months at the orphanage before going out into the wide world. The orphanage was run like a family home, where each of us had different duties to carry out each week, on a rota system. It was very democratically run by a man and wife team, who were wonderful - caring of our individual needs but firm where required. I enjoyed my life with them. There were twelve of us boys, an exclusive gang that no one else in the school could join: the Springhill boys. We stuck together as a team, and most of us joined the Scouts. I got to be Patrol Leader in our troop, and we often went away to places like Dawlish Warren and Portland Bill on Scout outings, but I was stripped of all my badges, lost my rank and was thrown out of the Scouts, for interfering with my best friend. In my mind, I hadn't done anything wrong; I wanted to be close to him and was expressing my affection in the only way I knew.

Although I was outwardly one of the gang, inwardly I saw the boys through different eyes. I did not like most of them overmuch, but I could very easily have loved two of them. The two who had a place in my heart were both black, and outsiders like me. The rest of the boys were part of another world. I was not much liked at the orphanage, after that, but no one bothered to investigate why I was like I was. It didn't spoil my feelings for the place, or those in it; I was eventually the oldest one there and gained some privileges. I spent my five shillings weekly pocket money on construction kits and things to build, then flew the kit aeroplanes that I built. The little dolls that I once dressed, together with Doreen, weren't to be found here, so I had to content myself with boyish pursuits, and fell into the mould of boyhood that the place instilled. By now, I had my own small bedroom, and would often masturbate into a container and waited patiently for the eggs to hatch out into little babies. I had read that babies came from eggs, and I totally expected mine to hatch. Any idea of sexual pleasure was as far away as it possibly could have been, I just had a deep wish to see my own eggs hatch and grow. I was left totally confused as to why it never happened, and eventually gave up the quest. I had at that time, even though I was now thirteen years of age, no idea of differentiation between male and female. I knew there were boys and girls and thought that babies somehow came from both.

One day, I was taken to meet an elegant lady who I was told was my new aunt. Apparently, there had been an advertisement in the national newspaper, the Sunday Pictorial, for aunts and uncles for orphans, and I was one of the lucky ones to get a new aunt and uncle. They were fantastic. Aunt Greta was quite tall, with beautiful blonde hair which she wore tied up on the top of her head in a most sophisticated way. She walked with a lightness of movement that I had never seen in any other woman, and had long slender fingers, with beautifully manicured nails. She dabbled in amateur dramatics and had such poise, and I wished she could be my new mum. Uncle Clive was a quiet, even-tempered man with greying hair and a very clean complexion. It was obvious that Aunt Greta and Uncle Clive had a reasonably comfortable life. They owned a timber yard and the smell there was lovely. I was allowed away from the orphanage on Sundays, to visit them for the day, and it was hoped that I would take on some of their finer attributes. On my arrival at the door, my Aunt Greta would inspect my hands, and more closely my fingernails, which were terribly dirty and misshapen. The first thing I learned from her was how to manicure my nails, so I would sit and file them, push the quicks back and polish them till they gradually became perfect. That is how I kept them, especially for Aunt Greta.

After the lesson in nail care, she would allow me to polish the big copper warming pan that hung on the living room wall, over the sofa. It was a lovely house, quiet and clean, without being clinical, a proper family home. Uncle Clive would take me on trips to the Cornish countryside in their car. Previously, they had a Lanchester but had replaced it with a Daimler Consort, which was a beauty to ride in. Going down the hill you could feel the weight of the car as it sped along. It was a huge car, and the only sound it made was the ticking of its clock. It had a preselect gear change and I was fascinated by the way Uncle Clive pushed the lever up or down as required and sometime later pressed the pedal on the floor.

I made a periscope to enable me to watch the birds in the cemetery next to the timber yard. I knew every bird in the place, where the nests were and how many chicks or eggs they each had. It was wonderful and I felt as if it was all mine. One Sunday, when I went to look at the birds, every one of the eggs had been smashed. I was devastated and felt I had led the killer to my treasure just by knowing where the nests were. After that, there was only the wood yard to look at, but I was very near to leaving the orphanage anyway. I missed my Aunt Greta and Uncle Clive, who showed a genuine care for me that I had not known for a long time. When, further down the line, I disgraced myself by being thrown out of the Army, they ended their relationship with me, and although I tried to communicate with them in later years, nothing ever came of it. I was very sad about the whole thing. My police record notes my 'well manicured hands', which was a legacy that I was never to forget, and I wish I could have fulfilled their faith in me.

When I eventually left the home that had been my security for the last year of school, I went to work in Bath and stayed in what was called a working boys' home. It was run by an ex Colonel. Any military bite that he once had was now gone. Although he was still very firm and had certain rules that we obeyed, he wasn't nasty.

There was a turkey farm just up the road, and at Christmas time they did a lot of killing. In the library at the house there was a book about Indian crafts, so from the hundreds of feathers that I brought back from the farm, I made the orphanage owner's son an enormous war bonnet. It was a major piece of work and took about six weeks to make, with its hand embroidered bead work band for the forehead, and leather thong tassels at the sides. It reached right to the floor and I doubt if he ever got to play with it properly because of its length, as he was only about six at the time.

I worked in a pie factory, with its own slaughterhouse on the ground floor and the main bakery on the first floor. Every morning, we would have to clock in, but to reach the time clock would mean running the gauntlet of the pig entrails that hung in the way. They would hang a pig, lungs and heart intact and covered in veins, with a hook right through its voice box, and its liver almost reaching the floor. It was absolutely revolting, but I still wanted to look at it all, and understand it, surgery and anatomy remaining one of my great interests.

The men worked on the ovens below, and the girls and I worked in the bakery above. We would fill the pie cases with the mashed meat that spewed from the machine, the right amount for each pie. Some of the things the men did with the body parts were disgusting, and I avoided them, glad to be with the girls, and not with those horrible men downstairs. I fell in love with a girl named Sally; the fact that she was married didn't mean a thing. The women teased me mercilessly, saying things like, 'Sally's waiting for you outside, she wants a date with you,' but they never hurt my feelings. I was young and innocent, life was a glittering crystal before me.

However, my attraction to females and weakness for men put me in emotional limbo. I was very aware of my lack of manliness, and my feminine spirit made itself strongly felt at times, especially in my contact with certain men. I knew I wanted to be more than just a bed mate for them, but did not have the domestic education that most girls had from an early age. This left me at a distinct disadvantage, and my awareness that I couldn't bear children made me put distance between myself and some men because of a sense of absolute inferiority and uselessness. The frustration of not having my own vagina drove me at times to utter distraction, and I despaired of ever feeling balanced and complete.

My stay in Bath lasted for three months. Most of the time was spent working, but I did go on the occasional ride on a very heavy bike that I had taken from the home. On my way to work in the mornings, I would ride down the Bathwick Hill at great speed, and in the evening, after work, climb that tortuous, mountain-like hill, an extremely tiring exercise. My time at the home was peaceful, with many an evening spent in the library the old Colonel had put together. Then, still under the auspices of the Children's Department, it was time to return to Plymouth.

I was now introduced into my first board and lodgings. There was Gran, an exceptionally old, very friendly lady, then there was the mum, with the husband who suffered fits and would quite often fly into a terribly violent rage for little or no reason. At those times he had the strength of six men, and only his wife had the ability to control him. Then there was the son, twenty years of age, and a baker by trade. He eventually seduced me on a quiet afternoon when there was no one else in the house. He was tall, slim and muscular, with dark soft hair and a short moustache, a wonderful gentle lover who was fully appreciative of my body. This pattern repeated itself regularly up until the time I joined the army. It felt so natural to be made love to by him. He always treated me as the girl, and I responded as such. It was the way I knew things to be.

Although I had had some experience with girls, it was never the same as when I was with a man, but I carried my secret with me into every workplace, shying away from the other men and not mixing much. I sat on the fringes. They were a different breed, I sensed, with their own code of language and ideas, and it was very difficult for me to connect with them. I often felt I wanted to, but knew I couldn't hide my feelings for long enough to be accepted as what they understood to be a complete man.

I would sometimes sit and watch them in the quiet knowledge that I had been to bed with one of their kind, and wonder what would happen to me if they found out. So many times, I really wished I could be a 'normal' man like the rest, and not have to suffer the guilt and disturbing feelings I had. There came the occasional man to whom I could relate, but I only desired to be with him as a woman, to be made to feel the way I ought to feel, so couldn't have him near me. I invariably left the job, or simply moved on. It eventually became my way of survival, an emotional net that I sometimes needed to fall into, this feeling for other men. Women were fine for the lovely feelings they invoked in me in a motherly way, but the strength of a man's love was something completely different. This was a need that came from somewhere deep inside me, a need that I didn't understand. There was still an element of fragile innocence that went with me through to my army days, and until I reached my eighteenth year.

I joined the army in 1962, at the age of seventeen and a half, because I was too old for an apprenticeship and decided that the army was the only place for me to learn a trade. I wanted to be a motor mechanic, something I'd had some experience of a few years before, when I illegally owned and drove my first car, an old Austin Seven, followed by a Morris Eight. I trained with the R.E.M.E. (Royal Electrical and Mechanical Engineers) and hated every minute of it. The worst experience of all was the first time I went to the showers with all those naked males. There was no way I was going to expose my body in front of them all, let alone look at theirs. I felt dirty at the thought that they might know how

I felt at the sight of their bodies. I would wait for as long as possible until the absolute minimum of them were there before I would shower; I felt that my privacy was being intruded upon. I learned to run and jump but was generally made to feel quite useless; it seemed that the big boys were playing a bigger game of soldiers, with their manoeuvres and all the ridiculous saluting that went on. In my opinion, they were just a bunch of grown up kids playing at being men, and there was not a man amongst them. They didn't know what that was, they only knew how to be male. The army failed me for active service, due to my colour blindness, so I ended up on a typewriter for the rest of my time with them. I very quickly came to the realisation that army life was not for me, what with all the orders of the day and duty rosters, and to cap it all, the weaponry. I had not considered beforehand that one day I might have to kill someone on the field of battle, and have wondered ever since if the youngsters that join up think seriously about this aspect of the 'exciting' army life they intend to engage in. I soon became tired of the routine and sought my way out eleven months after first joining up, finding myself back on the streets.

I went to stay in Stepney, with a girl friend I had made whilst in the army. I was now nineteen, and as big as a barn door, training with weights every other evening, in the kitchen of the flat where my friend lived with her parents. There was no sex: in the whole of my time with her we never had the desire to get it together. I spent the best part of a year there, working on the ladders, cleaning windows. I never saw anything I shouldn't, through the windows, but it was a very dangerous job, clambering around on the nineteenth floor of a skyscraper in the city, with the cars below like dinky toys, and no safety belts of course.

There was almost a code that you didn't wear them, to show that you had the nerve; I *did* have the nerve. One day I climbed fourteen floors of scaffold on the outside of the lifts with a jerry can of tea in one hand. That took nerve! Looking back, I suppose I was proving my masculinity.

I went to work for a company that made molasses from raw cane sugar, in the East End of London, near the East India Docks. For fourteen hours a day, I carried bags of raw sugar, unloaded from a barge on the river below. I lifted each bag, containing one hundred and twelve pounds of sugar, with one arm, whilst holding a knife in my other hand, used to split the hessian sack, so I could tip its contents into a boiling vat. I worked with another boy and the two of us kept a lovely rhythm. We were, I must say, the best two in the place. We got our overtime paid in cash, so we were both happy.

When I eventually left London to return to Plymouth, there was a strained atmosphere whenever I visited any of my aunts. I knew I was considered a bad penny by my uncles, and only just tolerated. Once, when one of them refused me Christmas Dinner, my lovely Aunt Ann gave me half of hers. I would have preferred to leave, but she said Christmas was Christmas, and I was to be included.

Chapter 7. Moving On

It was then, in 1964, that I took to the travelling life, and with no anchor to hold me, the journey took me where it would. The whole adventure bordered at times on nightmare, starting in Torquay, through the acquaintance of a man and a girl, and developing at breakneck pace. As though I was in a train, hurtling through a glass tunnel, I lost touch with the outside. Life was speeding, with me as its hapless passenger. I seemed to be offered no choice in what was happening to me. On lonely nights, I wondered whether other people's lives were like mine, but there came no answers, just the speed of the journey. I have often listened to the songs of Leonard Cohen and wondered what he must have seen of life to be able to write the things that he did with such deep insight into the human condition.

I found myself living with a group of young people, in a big empty mansion house on the side of a hill. Every day, they would congregate in a particular café. When I first arrived there, I knew no one and sat for a day or two watching who was who. One day a man came into the café; all the other boys knew him as a queer and avoided him. I never knew the word queer, it meant nothing to me, I just wanted to be loved. His hair was black and sleek and no doubt his use of Macassar oil contributed to the rich dark colour of it. He went around the cafe´ asking each person in turn if they would like a coffee or something to eat; he eventually came to me and asked the same. I said yes to his question, which meant I got fed; then he asked if I wanted to come back to his house for an evening meal, so I went with him.

That night, I slept in a large double bed with silky sheets, in a room lit by soft wall lights. The man owned a building firm and was well off. He was also alone, so that made two of us. He made love to me gently, into the night, and in the morning, twenty pounds waited for me by the bed. It was a fortune in those days, probably a week's pay. For about three months I was paid for each night I slept with him; I was the only one of the boys that would do it and so was the only one to have any money. Naturally, they all wanted the money, but I told them that they would have to sleep with him to earn their own. They never did.

When I left Torquay to head back to Plymouth, I met one of the nurses from Moorhaven Hospital, where my Mother had been for so long. The nurse was called Gill, and she was a nymphomaniac; I was later to learn that this a very sad condition for the sufferer. We got close to each other, and our lovemaking knew no limit: if she needed to do it, I was there to do it with her. I suppose I felt the call to fill her need, a need that reflected the emptiness of my own desires. In later years, I felt very much like she did, never gaining any lasting satisfaction from the sexual act as a male; I was only really satisfied as a female. However, when I did go with a girl, my appetite was insatiable.

Sometime after leaving Torquay, in 1969, I was informed by my aunt that after sixteen years, my mother had finally been allowed home to Plymouth, to live her life in society. I went to visit her and her man friend, who had been with her for many years in the hospital. He was quiet natured and had a deep love and regard for my mother. They seemed very happy together, but it wasn't long before he had a heart attack and died. My mother was once again alone in the world. I hadn't visited her at the hospital since I was a child, and so didn't know her at all. It was a strange experience to sit for the first time as an adult with the woman that everyone called my mother, and I imagine it was hard for her to sit with her sisters and try to find the thread of her broken life. She had undergone a lobotomy and electro-convulsive therapy and seemed to me as though she viewed the world through a window, an isolation that matched my own separation from the world. Despite the treatment, she was an extremely nervous woman. Before lighting her cigarette, for instance, she would check several times that she was lighting the right end. It sometimes annoyed me, but I never said anything. She was highly strung - what she might say to strangers in the street, if she thought they looked at her, was unpredictable and made them look at her even more. Somehow, though, she managed to hold her life together, and was not without lovers.

Sex was still a main objective in her life, as it had been in her youth, but whether this was part of her search for love I don't really know. She was very demure and secretive concerning her contact with men. It was as though there was no one in her private life, but I knew differently, as I gradually got to meet some of them. One night I slept at her flat, in the room next to her bedroom. She had a man with her, and after their lovemaking, they started to quarrel. He walked out, and the flat went quiet. Sometime later, there was a bang on the floor in the next room. I got up to investigate and found my mother on the floor, having swallowed a bottle of sleeping pills. I lifted her head from the floor and looked at the face that said: 'Freddy, Freddy.' I realised she was slipping into unconsciousness and raced out into the night to phone an ambulance. When she recovered from the stomach pump they performed at the hospital, she cursed me for saving her life, and wished herself dead. I suppose it would have been kinder, in a way, to have watched her die that night as we lay together on the floor. We had that kind of relationship. I felt I understood the suffering she had gone through and was very sad for her. Considering my own life at the time, it seemed as though we walked in parallel lines of suffering and loneliness, this image serving to push me away from what we were: two people, one blood, together as strangers. Gradually, we got ourselves together again, and she carried on with her life while I got on with mine. We never lived together, and I could never relate to her as my mother; she was the sad woman that had borne me in her body. Although I loved her, it was the same love that one has for a dearest aunt.

Many of my Christmases were spent on the road, wandering from town to town in the bitter cold, looking at the softly lit windows of houses and feeling lonely beyond all emptiness. At that time, it was difficult to get back on to the ladder of society once you had fallen, not that today is any easier, just different. Six years were spent as a total outsider, sleeping where there was to sleep, eating what there was to eat. It meant that I often slept with different men to secure a bed for the night, mostly being picked up by men in cars, sometimes in cafés or by long distance lorry drivers. Contrary to popular belief, they are not all macho men. There was something warm and secretive about making love in a dark lay-by, on the bed in the back of a lorry cab, in stark contrast to selling yourself in a bed and breakfast and afterwards lying awake all night next to a sleeping stranger, in the hope that he wouldn't rob you.

Rarely, there came along someone you felt you could trust and stay with for longer than one night. Bob was one such man. It was about eleven at night, and as I walked the dark lonely road towards Dover, a car drove up behind me and stopped. The driver asked where I was going and if he could he give me a lift. I got in and we drove in the general direction of Dover. I had worked in a bakery to earn some small amount of money, and wanted to go Europe to try my hand at whatever might present itself. As we drove, we talked, and he laid his hand on my thigh. It was the normal thing to happen and I did nothing to remove it. After some minutes, he asked me if I would like to spend that night with him and go on in the morning. I agreed, and we ended up at his little house, a two-up-two-down cottage on the edge of a village called Hawkinge, in Kent. Bob was a gentle man, in his fifties. That night, he ran me a hot bath, undressed me and lifted me in. He washed my long hair, which he wanted me to cut, because it hung to the bottom of my shoulder blades, and didn't look boyish at all, but I resisted his request, and kept my hair long. After he had bathed me, I stood up in the bath and as the water ran out, he dried me down and covered me in talc. Then he carried me like a bride, to his bed, where he made the gentlest love to me for what seemed an eternity.

Bob was kind, considerate and loving, and over the next three or four days, before I left for Dover, spared me no effort. He told me that his wife had died and I can only think that I was her replacement. I wished in later years that I had known just what I had with him; if that had been so, I might never have left. I had been with men before, but never one like him. He loved me, and

I took it for granted, taking his love and throwing it in the air like ash in the wind. I saw Bob on a few occasions in the next couple of years, but always missed what he had to offer. I was upset for a long time when I learned that he had died, mourning the fact that I was never the wife he wanted so much.

One day, when I was sitting at the side of the road, waiting for a car to come along to take me to who knows where, for such was life at that time, there was, on the other side of the road, another traveller. At twenty-two, he was older than me, with sharp features and pale blonde hair that hung to his shoulders. Beside him was his dog, the loveliest and saddest dog in the world – a little white terrier that looked like a lamb when he was washed. The dog was called Scamp, and his owner was known as Jan. They were inseparable, travelling together, sharing a bed and eating the same food, even dog biscuits, when they had any. Jan asked if I had a light for his cigarette, self-rolled, as were mine, made from those that had been thrown away by others. We sat in the sun, with nowhere in particular to go, and drank each other's company. He had about him an irresistibility; he was young, strong and streetwise, and somewhere underneath the aggressive shell, developed as the result of a hard life, there was another person that I am sure he never knew was there. He'd had a good upbringing and was well mannered, especially towards females. I was drawn like a magnet, and even during his most violent drunken episodes, I could not turn my back on him. I fell quietly in love, although I dare not admit it to him or the world. I kept my distance in all matters of the heart, and the only thing that he knew of me at first, was that I was heavily into girls. Over the years, he noticed there was also another me, and when I occasionally went with a man, he said nothing, although always intimated that I should not approach him in the same way. I sensed the danger in the very thought of the act, and dutifully kept my distance, nurturing feelings for him for twenty-three years. As long as I was a man, I knew that I could never let him know how I felt for him. Over the years, and all through our travels together, we kept a healthy distance between us, but I know that in his arms I could have been all the women he ever wanted.

Chapter 8. Drugs

At one point, around 1965, I was spending a lot of time in London and Kingston, as well as working in restaurants and hotels up and down the country, washing dishes, which was all I was fit to do. I had first smoked hashish when I was seventeen, with a group of young people, at the back of some old buildings in Plymouth. The hash was a golden-brown crumbly substance that one of the others made into a cigarette. It had absolutely no effect on me, and I continued to smoke the ephedrine tablets we bought from Boots the Chemists, for a shilling a bottle - good, but lethal and made your heart race. My first real turn-on to drugs had been when I went to live in Torquay, this turn-on leading to my love affair with heroin. I was now taking various drugs and generally getting more and more out of touch with the real world. Strung out for a fix of heroin to start the day, in the mornings I would go into town to see if there was anyone there to score from. After an hour or so, I would have enough heroin to last until midday.

I moved into an old derelict house with five others, and we shared everything that came our way but never broke the law. We would work a twelve-hour shift at Lyon's bakery on a Friday night, transferring hot bread from the ovens into the huge great trolleys that stood waiting. For this work we each earned five pounds, which guaranteed our food for the week. We would all eat at the Ivy café, and when there was no more money, we would put it on the slate until the Saturday morning, when we would pay up from the previous night's work at the bakery.

In the evening, we would go into the town, sit around on the Church Green and defy the police to come there to search us. The Vicar had told them that the Green was sacred, and they were not allowed on it. We had all sorts of drugs, from opium to hashish to heroin, speed and morphine.

I had my own syringe, which I never shared with anyone; there was a lot of jaundice around at the time. I would mix the heroin tablets in cold water and carry them in a small glass phial. The syringe was made of glass and was my prized possession; it lived in a velvet-lined wooden box I made. Heroin provided me with the warmth and security of the womb, and we became partners, lovers if you like. Lying on my mattress in the tiny cottage we occupied, with my syringe, the needles of which were very fine and short in length, I would draw off the clear liquid from the phial and tie up my arm with a belt to raise the veins. Then I would carefully slide the needle into a fat vein, release the belt and slowly press the plunger. After the initial rush of heroin, the room came into focus again and I would flush the rest from the syringe and watch it turn red with my blood. One or two of the boys would flush three or four times for the fun of it. Heroin made my eyes heavy and the itches which travelled from the arms to the chest to the feet were lovely; then there was the sensation of heat, and speech would slow to a crawling whisper. I couldn't bear noise of any kind, and it took all the time in the world to complete a sentence. Every movement took all my energy and it was best not to move at all. I spent fifteen months in Kingston Upon Thames, fixing every day, along with the many others, going up to London to score speed or heroin or whatever there was, but mainly heroin. It was pure, from the hospital, where many bent doctors would over prescribe for the extra revenue it brought them. They had no conscience about it: if you had the money, you got the gear. At that time, it cost a pound a grain, and there were six pills to the grain. It was very easy to get a pill of heroin on the street, and it only meant asking six different junkies to give or sell a pill and pretty soon one had a grain of the stuff to go to bed with, only to leave you in the same mess in the morning. So, the days went by, and stretched into weeks and months. Between men and men and fix and fix, this roundabout almost killed me.

It took a police raid on the town to force the situation and drive everyone out. The last night in Kingston was spent in Richmond Park, under the biggest tree, beside Eddie, my best friend at the time. He was thin and girl-like, with clear skin, fine features and a quiet way. I harboured a secret desire for him, but he was almost too pure to touch. On waking in the morning, we were surrounded by inquisitive cows, some of which were licking our hair; it freaked me out completely, and I was afraid to move. Between us, we managed to light a cigarette and blow the smoke up their noses. They backed off and I suppose they were harmless enough, but at the time it didn't seem like it at all!

Christmas was fast approaching, and the goose was not very fat. I eagerly awaited the day I would go to London with Eddie, to stay with Clare and Donna. They were from Cleveland, Ohio, and were in London in the belief that they could trap Georgie Fame and Eric Burdon into marriage. Donna had a settlement of nine thousand dollars from her previous husband and was here to spend it. We met the two girls in Kensington High Street. They had been shopping and were loaded down, and as we passed by in the van, we made some comment about Clare. She wore a huge black leather coat that made her look twice her normal size; she was quite short, had long black hair, and looked like a big black beetle. Her sister, Donna, was completely different. She was tall, taller than me in her shoes, of slim build, with red hair and the most beautiful hazel brown eyes. She looked stunning, like a film star, in a long green suede coat trimmed with white fur. Clare and Donna invited us back to their flat at Queen's Gate, Kensington, expensive to rent, but they could afford it. We planned to meet up again at Christmas.

In the meantime, I sometimes stayed at my friend Eric's flat in London, and one evening, on our way back there, a white Rolls Royce passed us and parked in a side street. A well-dressed man got out of the car and opened the passenger door, from which stepped a most beautiful blonde woman. I remarked on her beauty, to Eric, but his only answer was: 'Yes, but it's a man.' I just couldn't believe a man could look so beautiful, and the image tugged at my stomach, the echoes of some memory reminding me of my wish to be as beautiful.

The weeks rolled by in a drug-filled haze, and when Christmas finally came, Eddie arrived in the van, to take us to London and to the girls. Although I hadn't seen them since our first meeting, Eddie had been 'working on them' whilst he travelled back and forth from London to Kingston. On the day of our arrival, the food had all been prepared and the only thing in short supply was a good dose of drugs. It was decided that one of us would go and score, but it meant a trip down to Kingston. Eddie was elected, as the only one who could drive, and off he went. When he returned, I was already in Donna's bed, and Clare had gone to her own. This went down like a ton of lead, but it was not to be changed, and during the next ten days, Donna and I rarely got out of that bed. We swam together in a world of each other's bodies, the scent of sex filling the room as we indulged ourselves to the limit, the smell of her sex on me satisfying the desire for her scent to be mine.

The other two brought us the occasional meal, but there wasn't much time for eating. Donna was wonderful! I was nineteen, and she was thirty-three. I have never had sex like that with any other woman. We were to have many other sessions together, at different locations in London and at her flat in Bournemouth. I was totally taken with her and tattooed her name on my arm in India ink with one of my hypodermic needles. When she eventually went back to America, she was pregnant, and I had damaged her insides. I really felt the loneliness of the world as I watched Donna's flight leave, and had to journey back to the City, alone. I sometimes wonder about my son in the States, and relate his situation in life to mine as a young man, lost, perhaps, and wondering about his father.

My heroin habit got so bad that I didn't eat at all, living almost exclusively on orange juice, which quickly came back again. It became a sport to drink the cold juice down and bring it back into a plastic bowl. There being no bile in the stomach it would taste just the same as when it went down. Looking back, it was disgusting, but life was like that at that time. Sometimes I would smoke hash alongside the heroin, or smoke the two together and go into a vivid dream-like state like that induced by opium.

Sex on heroin was a weird experience: orgasm was denied for hours and hours; beautiful waves ran up and down the body, over and over, and the orgasm would come and go without ending, until, when it did, it was all consuming. Between girls, there were many men. I loved them all and took from every one of them something more than just memories. There were the feelings that each of them evoked in me, which gave me comfort in my lonely nights and sometimes empty days; they brought sanity and order to a world of hunger, cold and loneliness; they often provided me with the only food I would see for many days, when there was no work to be had and no money in my pocket. Men afforded me the transient love and warmth I sought in the barren wilderness that was my life.

But I was not the only one living in that wilderness. At times, I ended up in the 'spikes' - reception centres in South London, where the dregs of humanity sought succour from the state. We were at the end of our tether and had finished up at the bottom of the society's pile. These places were like prisons. Upon entry, we stripped off our clothes, then we were examined for fleas, body lice and crabs and dusted over with some powder to kill any which might be there. We were examined for V.D. and upon being declared clean were reissued our clothing for the night. We then went into the huge Dickensian dining hall with its long wooden tables and benches, where all the flotsam and jetsam of the city streets had landed for the evening meal of thick sustaining soup, and doorstep slices of bread. Our beds were mattresses laid in rows on the floor, with a pile of blankets for each, hence the strictness of the medical examination for creepy crawlies. In the mornings there was no easy way out, and we stayed to clean the floors and tables and wash the porridge dishes from breakfast.

There were other places too, not so draconian, but squalid, where a hundred men would sleep in one large dormitory, on narrow beds, side by side. Boots or shoes were always kept under your pillow, you slept in your clothes, and it didn't pay to have any belongings, as there was a risk of them disappearing in the night. Life bordered on dangerous if one of the more aggressive inmates decided that he wanted what was yours. There was a smell of stale urine, where countless inmates had wet the bed or peed on the floor or over adjacent beds. The stench of urine and stale bodies was unbearable by morning, and it was a case of getting downstairs as quickly as possible. Breakfast invariably consisted of fried eggs and toast, and to be late meant the eggs were rubbery and disgustingly greasy. Back out on the street, it was in this state that you were supposed to find some prospective employer, a virtual impossibility, as your appearance made it patently obvious where you had come from, and the answer was always, 'no room at the inn.'

In this condition, I often went to visit my aunts and was turned away by my uncles for being dirty and socially useless, so would drift on again. It was a vicious circle from which some never found a way out, and for others ended only when they passed on in the night: another paupers grave, another lost soul. We carried the stigma with us, and so the cycle perpetuated itself. In a way I was lucky because of my youth, which meant I could travel and seek my way out in some other way or place. Sometimes I would get an odd job in a hotel or somewhere similar, where the prospect of a decent meal each day presented itself. These places didn't always offer live-in accommodation though, so it still meant sleeping rough in order to be near the food source and the pitifully meagre pay on offer. This was survival in a way that many in our society still know.

A most valued asset at these times was a girlfriend, who would at least keep you in touch with human warmth and kindness. When there was no girl, there was a man. The men seemed to have what I needed to keep me strong and reciprocal in my feelings, although I doubt I knew what it was to give love at that time; I think any love had been stifled by the struggle for survival. Wherever I went, the culmination of a visit was the inevitable journey to the 'local' Department of Health and Social Security (DHSS) office, some miles away, to receive the seven shillings per day allocated to the homeless masses, masses of the lost and lonely people society had produced by its negative attitude to the needy and often unskilled.

'Oh, let me take you by the hand,
and lead you through the streets of London...'

The words of 'Streets of London', by Ralph McTell, were the reality of what I saw and shared with young men and young women washed up on the barren shores of an intolerant society, where no real help was being offered. Occasionally, some lucky individual would benefit from a Christian soul, but life is a marketplace, where life is cheap and everything has its price.

Top row L to R: Mother c. 1940, Mother c. 1960.
Second row L to R: Freddy c. 1950, Freddy and foster family, Desborough Rd, St Judes c. 1955.
Bottom row L to R: Mother, Barbara, Freddy and Charlie c. 1971, Freddy c. 1953.

me when I was 23 sitting in the linden-grove at anthony house torpoint?

Top row L to R: Barbara c. 1978/9, Barbara & Sarah 1976/7
Second row L to R: Freddy, Plymouth 1969, Jan and Freddy, Kingston, c. 1965.
Bottom Row L to R: Freddy c. 1978/9, Freddy (& handwriting), Anthony House, Plymouth 1969.

Top row: Joy just after transition 1989.
Bottom row L to R: Sarah & Joy, Eastbourne 1989, Joy, Greece c. 1990.

Evening Herald, Friday, June 10, 1994

ANIMAL CHARITY IN A FLAP AS PIGEON HERO'S PHOTO FAILS TO REACH TARGET

A PHOTOGRAPH of Gustav the pigeon – who flew wartime missions during the D-Day offensive – put Plymouth charity officials in a flap when it failed to arrive by post.

The snapshot of Gustav was to take pride of place at the city centre PDSA shop in an exhibition featuring courageous animal winners of their own wartime "VC" the Dickin –medal.

But the all important picture sent from Telford to Plymouth nearly failed to arrive apparently due to a first class mix-up by the Royal Mail.

PDSA officials in Telford had correctly addressed the envelope and sent it by the special "next day" delivery service.

When it failed to arrive after a day and a half the officials raised the alarm and the picture was finally intercepted in Exeter on its way back to Telford.

The PDSA's publicity chief Hillary Nelson explained: "It seems the Royal Mail was sending it back having failed to make a delivery.

"It's a bit much when you think of everything Gustav had to go through getting his message back from France to Britain in 1944. He was on time."

A Royal Mail official said they were investigating what went wrong and apologised to the charity for the mix-up.

With Gustav's picture in place, the exhibition marking the 50th anniversary of D-Day went ahead on time. It also included a picture of Simon, the only cat ever to win the animal VC.

He won it for bravery under fire aboard the Plymouth-based frigate Amethyst during the Yangtse Incident.

A volunteer at the shop shows her dog Charlie the Dickin Medal

Top row L to R: Freddy, Barbara & Sarah c. 1976, Barbara, Sarah & Joy at Sarah's graduation 1996.
Second row: Joy & Charlie, Plymouth Evening Herald 1994.
Bottom row L to R: Mary & Hilary 1988, Sarah and Joy 2016.

Chapter 9. Pilgrim

Once, when I was travelling, I got a lift in what I think was a Daimler or a Bentley. It was the middle of the countryside, and a most unlikely place for a car to stop, especially one of that calibre. The driver, a distinguished looking man of around fifty years of age, asked where I was going, and I gave him the standard answer: 'Nowhere special. Wherever you are.'

I got in, and we drove. The country looked lovely from inside that car, it reminded me of the trips to Cornwall with my Uncle George. We were talking about all sorts of things and it eventually got around to sex. He told me he had always harboured the wish to be whipped or caned like a naughty schoolboy! I didn't know what to say or do, never having come across this sort of thing before. I wasn't afraid, just puzzled as to what he was after. He then asked me if I would mind caning him then and there, and said he would pay me if I liked. It was the strangest request I have ever had made of me; I agreed to do it for him, if that was what he wanted, in order to give him some peace. He stopped the car at the side of the road and we both got out, and from the large boot he removed a case. In the case there were school-type canes; he asked me to choose one, then we walked to the front of the car and he lay over the wing, right there in the roadway. I stood to one side of him and didn't know exactly what to do until he asked me, with emphatic voice, to beat him. I took the first stroke, almost afraid to hurt him, but he begged me to hit him harder, and even harder. Soon, I was hitting him with all my might, to the rhythm of his begging. After some minutes of this thrashing, he quietly asked me to stop, and took the small case back to the boot. He never once tried to touch me sexually or made any reference to it. He thanked me, and after a short distance in the car, gave me some money and let me out to go on my way.

If you lived from day to day and took life as it came, it offered plenty of opportunities to live or to die, depending on the day. In Greece, a man who wanted my girl tried to run us down on the roadside when he found he couldn't have her. We had taken a lift, and after driving for some distance the driver pulled off the road into what looked like an old aircraft hangar. Inside, there were three or four other men who closed the huge door behind us. I told my girl to make her way to a small door at the side of the building, and I followed close behind with the seven-inch knife I always carried. Once on the road again, we walked as fast as possible away from the place, but suddenly, behind us, on the grass verge, came the same car again. We had to jump out of the way as it scythed the grass verge where we had been; thankfully, it didn't come back. My girl told me how, whilst I slept in the front of the car, the driver had reached over into the back seat as he drove and put his hand between her legs. He stopped when she bit him, but she didn't wake me for fear of what I might do with that knife. Knife or no knife I was still afraid of confrontation and while an aggressive stance was to remain my best protection, it was an empty threat, as inside I was still timid, and afraid of men.

Another time, a man wanted to push a bottle in my face to incapacitate me and take my girl, while others tried to get me drunk and take her that way. Some of the men who tried for her were lovely, and I sometimes envied her for the men she attracted. Inside, I was saying, 'Look, I'm here, too!' but of course, to them, I was just another man and not at all what they wanted.

Some of the men *did* want me. While staying as a visitor in a flat in Holland, a male nurse and his male wife tried to seduce me on the sofa, but I was young and a bit nervous about having two of them at one time, so eventually they gave up and I was allowed to sleep on the other sofa.

I made my way up through Germany, Denmark and Sweden, arriving in Oslo in August 1966. It was there I met Jorunn. She was like an angel and very pretty, and would meet me every day after her work, give me cigarettes and take me back to her parents' cottage, whilst they were on holiday in Sweden. I would go for a bath, and Jorunn would bring joica - tinned reindeer meat balls, which formed my staple diet. During the day, whilst she was at work, I would mix with people from all over Europe, and as far away as Japan. There were two Japanese travellers who had cycled the whole way!

One night, I was sitting in a shop doorway with a group of youngsters, playing guitar and singing. A drunk approached us and asked if we would like to go back to his place. We all agreed and got on the tram with him, travelling to his flat at the end of the line. Once in the flat, everyone else went into the living room, but I made it clear that I would like to use his bath. There I was, languishing in the bath, when there was an almighty commotion in the passageway as he realised that it was a houseful of boys, not girls, he had got for the night. It was an easy mistake to make, as we all wore our hair down our backs and were young and pretty. We ran down the stairs into the street, me still clutching an armful of clothes and wringing wet from my unfinished bath, whilst he shouted behind us that he would call the police. It was a long walk back to Oslo along the tram tracks.

It was in Oslo, from the top of the Ekeberg campsite, that I witnessed the Aurora Borealis, or Northern Lights. It was fantastic, like a huge cinema curtain hanging in the sky, from top to bottom and side to side of the horizon. It moved up and down at its lower edge and in and out like silk. The colours were amazing - pale blues, pinks and oranges. I had seen a similar effect whilst in the mountains near a place called Voss, where there was a huge waterfall. On that occasion, we were all stoned on cannabis and stopped the car to sit and watch the colours as they perpetually changed, in small patches, like clouds.

While we were in Oslo, the friend that I had travelled with had journeyed to Istanbul to buy opium, but was only able to bring back some hash. This was very quickly dispensed with, and he went off to Istanbul again. Meanwhile, I lived with Jorunn in the cottage, and very comfortable it was, too. There were many parties on the fjord, in people's houses and in the woods. One house we stayed at was in the middle of the forest, and was built of logs, with a wooden roof covered in moss. Every morning, a squirrel would come right into the house to get its breakfast.

Two Americans, who had been demobbed in Kaiserslautern in the south of Germany, had made their way to Oslo by car, every cavity filled with different types of hashish. With them came Katja. She had the typical long blonde hair of the North, combined with a slender figure, and it was she who was to accompany me on the way to Spain, at the beginning of October, when the Norwegian winter was about to set in.

In Almeria, Katja and I sat in a park, watching a little man who stood with his box and sold single cigarettes and packs of sunflower seeds. He had very little, and we had even less; we were waiting for some money to arrive from Bob, in England. As we sat there in the afternoon sun, a woman of about thirty years of age, with long black hair, sat beside us. She had taken a liking to my blond hair, which was almost to my waist and shone like spun gold in the Spanish sunshine. Communication was impossible, as we spoke no Spanish and she spoke no English. She pointed in the general direction of my private parts and said 'negra' which means black, in Spanish. I tried to tell her that the hair there was the same colour as that on my head, but she insisted it was black. She beckoned us to go with her, so we followed the woman to a narrow street, on each side of which were equally narrow doorways, and standing in nearly every one of them was a man. At each door she would stop, and the bartering would start. It became clear to us that she was attempting to sell Katja to one of the men in order to pay for the privilege of seeing my naked blond-haired body for herself. Once it became obvious to her that it was not what we wanted, she took us to a café and bought us food that we could barely manage, having eaten so very little in the past few weeks. We ate some out of politeness and went back into the town to wait for the money from England.

When the money finally arrived, we went to the bank to change the pound notes into pesetas. The bank was crawling with armed guards and it struck me as funny that so many were needed to protect individually worthless pesetas. We went back to the little man in the park and bought some cigarettes from him as a token of our thanks for the gifts he had given us over the previous two days. Katja and I had begun to argue, and it was time for us to part company, so she left for Morocco with a group of Danish boys. On my way back to England, I met a French boy who had brought a half kilo of cannabis into Spain with him, so we ended up under the flood bridges in Valencia, catching rats with our sleeping bags at night. He spoke six languages and was funny to be with, and I stayed with him as far as Barcelona, before making my way slowly back to England.

Chapter 10. Homemaker

Lizzie was a mousy haired girl of Scottish origin. She was very well educated and spoke French and Russian. I met her at the house of a friend, an artist of quite some ability. The house was full of paintings, some of them of a very disturbing nature, such as the insides of people and animals in colour. Vivid in their depiction of death. I had rented a flat in the attic of a large house, where I lived with my cat - I had always loved cats. I invited Lizzie back to my castle in the sky and for days we never saw the streets. We made love continuously, day and night, stopping only to eat and drink. We cut the world out of our lives for that wonderful time together, and were in love, or so it seemed. Lizzie and I decided to live in London, so we went to a commune in Chiswick. They were lovely times - walking in the quiet cemetery during the day and jumping on the tube into the City for the night. I was happy to have found someone to reflect my feelings and nature, permanently so I thought, someone I could relate to.

My mother desperately wanted me to get married, although this was far from my mind at that time. I had never given it a thought, but she worked liked water on a stone, and in the end, I asked Lizzie if we should. We had been together for three months before the fateful day, and on the occasion of our marriage, I thought that at last I perhaps did have everything that a man could want. We decided to return to Plymouth, and found a furnished flat in the vicinity of the dockyard, made up of a kitchen, small lounge and bedroom. In one of the cupboards we found an old bracelet, made from plaited human hair, with a pinchbeck clasp and five large amethysts. It was a strange thing to find at the bottom of the cupboard, an omen, perhaps, as it turned out to be a Victorian mourning bracelet, which duly got sold so we could buy things for our home.

At the front of the house there was a small garden, with a long lavender bush along its edge, a sprig of which was always in the flat. At the back of the house there was an orange blossom tree, and when it was in bloom I would bring Lizzie some of the blossom to dot around, to make the place look attractive and cast scent about the room. It was my way of giving her nature's love and beauty.

On Sundays, I would play the music of Beethoven and Mozart out through the window. On one such day, we decided to mow the grass. When it was all finished and it was time to collect up the grass, there was a cry from my wife as she discovered that her wedding ring was missing; it had gone through the mower! I found it eventually, in five pieces, and went to an Australian friend of mine who put the ring together again, so you wouldn't have known it had ever been through a mower.

I had no work, no skills, nothing that would secure us a decent means of living. We only had each other, but we contacted old friends and life went on its way. Then came November and bonfire time, and the streets were full of children collecting furniture and wood for the fires. Our little flat was furnished, but we wanted to get our own home together, and there was a sudden wealth of furnishing in the streets: a thousand and one things from the past. We collected inlaid tables, chairs, chaise longues and old lace curtains until the flat was full of the stuff. We didn't have a clue what it was we had, but it was clean and solidly made. I had no idea of period or wood, and we treated it as ordinary furniture to live with; little did we know that it was being more and more sought after by antique dealers, and there we were with enough to fill five rooms. It was from almost every period of English history and cost us nothing but a few fireworks for the kids. I began to learn about English antiques and their origins, to recognise different woods and types of inlay. After some time spent cleaning and re-covering items, I became quite skilled and slowly developed a trade to which I could turn. I started upholstery classes at the Swarthmore Institute and learned to strip out the old upholstery, rebuild it to its original condition and transform the furniture pieces into works of art. Eventually, I started to do work for antique shops, and began to make good contacts in the trade. In the window of one shop, I spotted a chair just like the one I had at home and went in to ask if they wanted another one the same - I had soon sold my first antique.

The collection grew and our home took on the appearance of a museum. With its lovely lace curtains, cane chairs and Honduras mahogany table, with massive claw feet and huge centre pillar supporting its enormous top, it was like walking into the past. The picture rail was hung with dozens of ribbon plates, threaded through with coloured ribbons. There were numerous variously coloured hot water bottles on the sideboard and smaller tables, and in the small bedroom there was a lovely mahogany bed, and the most beautiful dressing table with shaped front, cabriole legs and shaped mirror over the top, surmounting the tiny drawers that held my wife's belongings. There were little china ornaments and carved ivory pieces dotted about, and old pictures in dark frames hung on the walls. At last it seemed that life had released its hold on me, and that I could settle down into some semblance of normality – but that wasn't to be so.

I was working a permanent night shift on the railway, and damned hard work it was too, twelve hours every night, getting home at six in the morning. One morning, I came into the street where we lived and knew from where I stood at the bottom of the road that our home was empty. Lizzie had gone. My world fell into a thousand pieces, I just could not believe it had happened. What had I done wrong? I had worked long and hard and had, at last, a way to bring us things we both wanted. She had burst my world like a bubble. It seemed as if the episodes with the mourning bracelet and broken wedding ring had been omens of a sort. I wandered for days in a trance-like state, and searched everywhere for her, but she was nowhere to be found, having run off with the artist through whom we had met. I was alone again. The mirror image of my real self had gone from me and I lost myself, falling into a deep depression. My emotional doors shut, and there seemed nothing left to live for, until Barbara came into my life.

Chapter 11. Barbara

Barbara is, in my memory, the only person since my first 'mum' and Aunt Ann to have loved me unselfishly, without condition or reserve. She was in my life when all others disappeared. No greater love have I had. I loved her beyond measure, and yet I plucked the petals from the flower and caged her wild spark of life in a prison of my jealousy. I did my best to ensure that no one took her from me, but I was not fit or worthy of her.

Barbara was a small girl, aged seventeen, with a heart-shaped face, and an awkward way of standing which gave her an individuality that everyone knew. Her long blonde hair stretched down her back. She was beautiful. I had known her for some time while I was with Lizzie, and after Lizzie left, asked if she would come to the house and cook me some food as I was terrible at it. I was still working, and one morning I came home late to find her with her back to me, cleaning the stairs. I knew then that I had to have this girl for my own. She had been invited on a boat trip that day, but decided to stay with me. We lived and loved and gradually merged as one entity, travelling on the same road together in life, then one day I asked her if she would like to go to Istanbul. We sold everything, got our passports and went to say our goodbyes to Bob, my one-time lover.

Barbara had only a visitor's passport, and wasn't allowed into the Iron Curtain countries, so we travelled down through Belgium into Germany and Austria over the Alps and through the Brenner Pass into Italy. The Alps are beautiful at night, and as we walked through the Brenner Pass the mountains stretched upwards to such a height that the foreshortening effect made them look stunted. The roadway stretched into the distance and the whole scene looked like a picture postcard. The houses and church in the little village of Mittenwald had shutters painted on the walls, and the church tower had imitation joints between bricks, painted to resemble pointing.

On the outskirts, there was a shrine, where you could light a candle and say a prayer. It was very beautiful, and Barbara loved it. As evening crept in, it was lucky for us that a car came along and took us to a place where we could catch a train into Innsbruck, which lay in the bottom of a deep valley, and from there we caught the train into Italy.

Most of the time, we hitchhiked, and met many different people on the way. In Italy, we met Chas, an older man, and spent three days and nights travelling the whole length of Italy in his lorry. At Brindisi, we caught the ferry to Greece, then journeyed up through Greece, through Thessalonica and on into Turkey, meeting the local villagers and gypsies, who were very friendly and treated us as fellow travellers.

Late in the afternoon, on one of those long days, it became very dark, and heavy thunder clouds gathered overhead. Slowly at first, the heavy raindrops began to fall on us, gathering pace until the sky was a solid sheet of water. It was now pitch black, and we were in the middle of the countryside, with no apparent shelter from the deluge. Some distance away, through the darkness and the rain, we saw a small light, and tortuously made our way towards it. As lightening flashed, we could make out the shape of railway trucks standing in the sidings, and a huge barn-like building, from which came the tiny light we had seen.

By now, our clothes were stuck to our bodies, but you learn that, on the road, daylight is for making new acquaintances and not the middle of the night, so a large railway truck with its loading side down afforded us some shelter from the driving rain, and we waited until morning to find out what the light was.

Morning broke to reveal a clear sky, and from the direction of the barn there came the sound of children and adults talking. We made our way over to the entrance of the building. Inside, was a family or two of Turkish gypsies, who had erected a large tent. The walls of the barn threatened to cave in at any moment, large pieces of plaster propelling themselves into the middle every now and then. There they all were, women, men, and chickens, amongst little children still in their beds. The light we had seen was from the fire they had lit in the middle of the tent. We had with us a bottle of Johnny Walker, and I offered it to the man who stood nearest to us. He took a drink from the bottle and it made its way round the tent to everyone there, children and all. We ate Turkish bread and goat's cheese with them and watched them pack up the tent and disappear, the men on bicycles with baskets, to sell combs and small things on their journey. They gave us a comb as a souvenir, but it got lost, as most things do when one travels.

Once inside Turkey, we turned south, and travelled down to the ruined city of Ephesus, and the temple of Diana. Although the main ruins had an enormous wire fence all around them, there was plenty to see outside. We found an amphitheatre which wasn't in too bad a condition. Built high in the outer surface of its thick walls were little cells, the entrances to which were about the size of a man. The cells were round and funnel-shaped to the floor, with brick-lined ceilings. From the doorway, if that was what it was, we could see out over the countryside, and at night we would light a fire and listen to a shepherd singing in the fields below, and the little bells on the necks of the sheep would jangle and jingle. There was no chimney for the smoke to escape, and we were entirely black from it. During the day, we would go up to the entrance of the theatre, to lie in the sun and clear dust from areas of the beautiful mosaic floors that had been hidden for so long. It was magical.

After two or three days, we travelled northwards again, first towards Ankara, and finally Istanbul. Istanbul was a city of minarets and markets, where the cemetery had tombstones with funny hats, according to the rank of the dead occupant. The Grand Bazaar had a thousand shops, and all along the Bosphorus strait, little fishing boats sold fresh fish fried on braziers. The air was blue with smoke from charcoal burners. At night, there were sellers of hot chestnuts on the street, and in the heat of the daytime sun there were bottles of sterile water to drink. Turkish Delight wasn't as we know it in England, but was sweet cake kept in refrigerated cabinets. The cigarettes were terrible and fell to pieces as you took them from their thin paper packs.

We stayed in the hotel Gulhane, where, on hot nights, travellers would sleep up on the roof for less than the cost of a room. There were dire warnings of what would happen to you if you smoked hashish while there: thirty years jail for Europeans. We once went to stay the night with the lady who cleaned the hotel, who kept a rooster in the outside toilet. Turkish tapestries were hung on the walls and draped over the bed. She had three very shy daughters, with jet black hair, who were intrigued by us and giggled all the time. They were a lovely happy family. The Turkish men liked Barbara's long blonde hair and slight figure, and on a few occasions, I had to stop myself from going after one or two of them that had grabbed a handful of her anatomy. They were like bees round a honey pot.

Soon we ran out of money, and stood at the gateway to the East with only two English pounds in our pockets, our rare two dollar bill having been spent in the grand Bazaar, to buy Barbara a sheepskin jacket which stank to high heaven on our return to Europe, even though it was winter! I also bought her a lovely gold puzzle ring, which was later stolen from us in England, during a break in. The two English pounds were to be our saving grace. We put an advert in the pudding shop, to attract the attention of anyone going to Europe, but of course, everyone wanted to go on to India, so we spent days waiting to get out of Istanbul. Then one morning there was an advert for passengers to Europe. There was a convoy of two cars going to Germany, so with our last two pounds we got aboard a Mercedes Benz, which the young owner had brought to Istanbul to sell as a taxi but was too small, as the Turks ran huge fifties style American limousines, some with running boards which the passengers would stand on and be whisked through the streets at an alarming pace. The traffic cops had no authority at all, arms waving about meaninglessly, it was all very amusing. Amongst the chaos were thousands of stray cats. They were everywhere, asleep on walls and street corners, just everywhere.

We were on our way back to Europe, in the Mercedes, accompanied by five others. There was one German couple, one Canadian couple and an Arab who no one liked because he shared nothing with the rest of us, and to share was survival. In Greece, we tried to sell our blood, at the going rate of fourteen dollars a pint. They didn't want mine though, as they said I looked like a drug addict. They weren't far wrong, although that was in the past. They also said that because of Barbara's small size she had less than the normal amount of blood in her body, which made us all laugh.

It was decided that, because of the small amount of money we had between us, we would travel through Yugoslavia instead of crossing to Italy on the ferry. This created a problem, as Barbara, you remember, had only a visitor's pass, so would not be allowed to enter Yugoslavia. However, my pass included a photo of my previous wife, so the solution was for Barbara to travel as my wife. We drove up to the border and one of the guards took all our passes to the police hut some yards away, all that is, except Barbara's. The wait seemed endless. Then they came back, handed over the passes, and we drove on. It worked. We had done the same thing into Italy, Greece and Turkey. I had wanted to see if it was possible to pass her off as Lizzie; they just seemed to see a man and a woman, and that was enough. So here we were in Yugoslavia, free as birds. We had a limited amount of food for the journey and rationed ourselves accordingly. The Arab had a box of chocolates, and he surprised us by giving everyone in the car a chocolate. But before we had time to enjoy this unexpected gift, our lives were almost taken from us.

We were on a three-lane highway, where the centre lane was the overtaking lane for both streams of traffic. In the far lane was a vehicle that was being overtaken in the centre by another car, and in our lane was another car overtaking him. There was nowhere to go, as on our right side was a deep ditch and a field. We slowed as much as possible and got down behind the seat. Barbara and I were fortunately in the back. There was an almighty crash and the other car hit us head on, one of its passengers being thrown right through the windscreen and landing on our bonnet. The Arab was smashed into the windscreen of our car, and the driver and the third person in the front were thrown onto the steering wheel. It felt as though the front seat was wrapped around my chest, but it only bruised my ribs. How the impact didn't kill anyone, I do not know. The injured passengers were whipped off to hospital and we continued our journey to Lubiana, with the car loaded on the back of a breakdown truck!

The only thing that worked in the car was the radio, so we played it at full volume with the windows wound down, as we travelled through the streets, with the shopping crowds watching us as though we were from outer space. Fortunately, both cars were German and insured with the same company - so we found ourselves the guests at a four-star hotel for the weekend, paid for by the insurance company. At the end of the weekend we were issued with second class tickets on the Trans-Europ Express, to the destination of the vehicle, which was Bremen, and so it was that we travelled into Germany for free. One of the others lived in Ulm and invited us to stay there for Christmas, but we stayed only a short while, and moved on to Heidenheim.

On entering the village, we were met with the most wonderfully sweet-scented air, the effect of which wore off after a few hours. The shops in the little streets were of typical Bavarian style. The framework of one had painted sweets and sticks of candy from floor to gable, and right in the point of the roof there was the face of an old witch. It was Hansel and Gretel's sweet house! In the evening we would go to the music house on the edge of the Black Forest, to listen to very loud music, or would sit among the roots of the trees some hundred yards away and listen to the music as it drifted across the snow in the darkness. The snow was very deep, and the trees must have been hundreds of years old. There we would sit and smoke hash, entirely one with nature.

Whilst visiting Ulm, I contracted what is known in Europe as the Grippe. This is a particularly vicious form of the flu virus, and that winter, people were dying of it all over Germany. I was in a coma for three days and only survived because of the kindness and care of Jochan, whose father was the village doctor. We had no means of paying for medicine. He was my saviour. After my recovery, we spent Christmas in Heidenheim, entertained by our friend's dear old Yugoslavian grandmother, who taught us how to make stuffed green peppers, a typical Yugoslavian dish. She was a very small woman, who tied her hair in a bun and walked with a stoop, bent almost double, muttering to herself the whole day long.

Chapter 12. Stirrings

We were away for ten weeks, arriving back in England in the New Year and making our way to Plymouth, where we lived at first under terrible conditions, in flats with separately rented toilets. Slowly, we managed to climb the social ladder and eventually were able to get a nice flat and furnish it mainly with antiques, once again found or bought cheaply from sale rooms. Life began to settle into a normal pattern, but underneath, the ghosts from the past were stirring in my breast. We married, and in 1972, Barbara gave birth to a daughter. She was beautiful as a baby and is the pride of my life. In those early days there seemed to be nothing to mar a lovely family such as ours. We had met a young couple in Plymouth and became very friendly, but they were to return to Germany, which was the girl's homeland. We sat and discussed the possibility of us going over to join them, and it was agreed that they would go first, to get settled, and we would follow them later.

So, in 1976, we sold up and moved on again, taking the best of all we had to Germany, in five crates. For the first few weeks, we lived with our friends, but their little boy was one of the worst behaved children that I have had the misfortune to meet, with absolutely no manners, and life became unbearable. We left their house with nowhere to go and ended up in the bed of a friend we had made there. He was from Burma, one of two brothers seeking political asylum. They worked the night shift in a plastics factory near Stadtmitte Station. It was a bed that we otherwise would never have had, as neither of us spoke German, and we didn't know our way around the system. We would have come home to England, had it been possible, but our complete home was on a ship, in the crates.

I found work in a small factory, machining wood for the kitchen industry. My boss was our guardian angel and arranged for us to move into the second floor of a beautiful house, right in the middle of the small town of Bad Salzuflen. The house was of oak framed construction, with foot square beams inside and out. Inscribed with the date 1627, it was the second oldest house in the town, and had a preservation order on it. The outside was painted, whilst the inside had been totally restored, with central heating and a beautifully fitted bathroom. It was very bright and airy, with two-way opening windows at the back and oak framed ones at the front, which were later double glazed against the winter cold. In winter the ice was half an inch thick on the inside of the windows, from our breathing in the night. We had seen the house during our few days of being in the town; it was one of those places that one longs to live in but that is usually reserved for the wealthy. In England, the chance would never have arisen, but at that time the Germans did not want to live in an old house, preferring something brand new and modern. The doors were very low, and many a visitor collected a bruise as a souvenir, where they struck the top of the door frame with a resounding thud on the head. I can only imagine we walked with a permanent stoop.

Then, in the factory where I worked, there was an accident. A machine ripped one of my fingers off and smashed two others. After ten days in the hospital, I spent a further four months at home, unable to use the hand at all. It took me months to tell everyone in England what had happened. In a twist of fate, my GP asked me what I had done in England, and I told him that I had worked with antiques. Apparently, a company in Bielefeld specialised in importing English antique furniture, and a few days later I went to see them. This was the turning point of our life in Germany. We all learned German, and I quickly became integrated with the work team and ended up in a very forward position in the workshops, on the restoration side of the business. Three years later, when the company changed hands and the new owner got too greedy, I opened my own little shop in Bad Salzuflen and took with me the customer lists from the old company, which ensured I had all the contacts I needed. I never earned a fortune, but we had our own car and enough to take us to England for Christmas.

Life was good in Bad Salzuflen. We made a lot of friends and spent many a summer's day on the farm, with our good friend Irena, walking through the golden cornfields and woods that were all around, eating the earthy walnuts that grew there. Evenings found us seated around the barbeque, and much wine and food was consumed until late, when the owls would call on the rolling hill. Corn waved in the breeze, like an ocean of gold, right up to the walls of the little farmhouses, and in September the tractors would fill the roads as they trundled along with their loads of sugar beet, much to the annoyance of the drivers behind them. The summers were beautiful with their sights and celebrations, and when the Kirmis came to town, the children would go to the woods and indulge themselves in all the fun of the fair.

Autumn was golden, but winters were long and very cold and hard, and everyone who could afford it wore their best fur coats and boots. On Sundays, after church, they would parade around the large lake in the park, showing off their wealth like so many stuffed bears. When the water froze to thick ice, the town turned up to ride bicycles, skate, ski and play ice hockey. The lake was about a half mile long and a quarter mile wide, with a small island in the middle, on which the ducks and swans would build their nests. Beyond the lake were the woods - deep pine forests, with snow all around. It was quite dry amongst the trees, because they were so densely planted. Signs warned of TOLLWUT (rabies), and you would occasionally find a poem painted on a shield, celebrating the Fuchstanz, the fox dance.

There was a shadow on the horizon. Since attending a party in England, one Christmas, the feelings roused by an encounter with a dress were not to leave me. We arrived in Plymouth and were invited to a fancy-dress party. My friend and I were to play the part of Cinderella's ugly sisters. On the night of the party, we went to get changed into the clothes the girls had set out for us to wear. No sooner had I dressed when a terrible feeling came over me. It was as though someone or something had wrapped itself around me, like a cocoon. I felt sick. Sick with anticipation. Sick with the strange pleasure that now enveloped my body. A ghost from way back in my dark past had alighted on me. It was as though I had always belonged there, and suddenly the dark figure of myself stood in the room to reclaim me after all those years of wandering and searching. I had no desire to go to the party. It was as if the whole room could see and sense the rightness that I felt while I stood there in that dress. The scales had tipped, and my balance felt exactly right, I was terrified but oddly secure. I didn't mention it to anyone. I was afraid to. I didn't know what they might think.

I'd had numerous affairs with men but had never considered myself to be 'queer', or 'gay'; it was just a normal part of living that I never questioned. But now, somehow, the door had been opened to another world. I realised that for all those years and to all those men I had been a wife, and that somewhere within me there lived some other being.

I tried to block it out in the best way that I could, with work, but eventually confided in a female friend of ours who gave me one of her dresses for my birthday, sprayed with her perfume. The dress was made of white cheesecloth and smelled lovely. I wore it on the rare occasions when my wife was not at home. My 'condition' was getting worse, but not outwardly obviously so. I started to look for men but did not know anywhere I could meet anyone. A friend and his wife would visit us on Friday evenings, and on occasions the husband and I would go out into Bielefeld, to the Kino, to watch a film or two. One night, out of the blue, we seemed to sense each other's need, and made love in the car on the way home. I was torn to pieces afterwards. It was something that I had not done for years. I couldn't get it out of my mind, and it never happened again with him. He was transferred back to England, as his posting had come to an end. It all finished very quickly but left its stain on me, as though I had touched something that I had forgotten about. Ghosts from the past called me from a great distance, echoing in my mind.

One weekend, we held a party at our place in Lange Strasse, Bad Salzuflen. It was crowded with friends from work and elsewhere, and among them was the boyfriend of one of the girls. I had loved him for a long time and felt jealous of her every time I saw them together. I could hardly bear to have him near me, the feeling was so strong. I would have loved to have him for my own, but buried my feelings deep, and showed nothing. On the night of the party, he got very drunk and fell through a shop window, cutting a vein in his head. He was in a bad way, covered in blood from head to foot. I took him into the bathroom and tried to clean him up a bit before the ambulance came. I had never been so near to him, and the feel of his skin on my hand, and the soft roundness of his muscles, made me want to take him in my arms and love him. I felt like a mother to him. It was more than a question of sex; I wanted to comfort and cradle him in order that he might sleep. I felt strongly protective, and was glad to have him to myself without the intrusion of the others to take away these wonderful feelings. How I managed to get us out of the bathroom and down into the street I don't know, but I did cradle him in my arms all the way to the hospital. It was beautiful, though afterwards I felt as if I had stolen something from him while he was at a disadvantage. I was covered in his blood and could smell the iron in it, strong and pungent. I kept those feelings as something very special, never hinting at them, even in the vaguest terms. There was a quietness about him that a lot of men didn't have, and although he could be difficult at times, it was only his way of wanting to be alone with himself. His girlfriend never seemed to see that, and I would get quietly angry inside with her, for taunting and teasing him in the cruel way she had, but I had to sit tight and bear it.

I couldn't understand or come to terms with the eternal war going on inside me. It made me permanently irritable and I was well known for my bad moods amongst our friends, as I desperately tried to hide the fact that there was anything bothering me. I put up a shield of masculinity that was very convincing, to protect me from the harsh reality of how I felt inside. How could I admit to the world and to my closest friends that I was anything but just like them? The reality of transsexualism was the slow insidiousness of its action on my soul, a rightful claiming, eating me like a mantis eats its prey. All consuming, it had stalked me from the age of seven and had now trapped me in a corner with nowhere left to run to, in Spain, Germany, or anywhere else. My real nature had at last caught up with me and proceeded to impose on my life.

I carried my male armour until I could go on no more with the weight of it. Then it was time to collapse with the strain of the part that I had played for so long. I was getting more and more tired. No one can imagine the guilty feelings generated by having to watch your wife and daughter love you and give of themselves, while all the time an animal wanders inside you and slowly eats your innards away until there is nothing left but the animal. I now knew I wanted a husband of my own, not to be one. I wanted to be able to share love with a man and be able to look at him and know that I wasn't like him. I needed to see the difference between us, and not always see myself in relation to a woman and be constantly reminded of what I felt myself to be. I needed a man to bounce off as my distinct opposite. The animal in my case was an imprisoned woman, a woman that had been locked inside me for many years. It took only the key of *that dress* to unlock the door and let her out. I fought the need to go and buy a dress of my own and felt physically sick each time I thought about it.

Life fell under a dark cloud; as each day dawned, the beast would wake with me and prowl quietly in my inner recesses. At times I didn't even notice it was there, and for a while I forgot it altogether and things seemed to go back to normal, but she had seen life now, and no inner prison was to hold her back. My torture was her screaming to be set free to live her rightful life, whatever that might be.

Chapter 13. Mother

In 1982, my family and I returned to England and stayed with my wife's parents for seven months, before moving into a small cottage we had bought - a lovely little place in the middle of the town, tucked away from the world and quite difficult to find. It had two bedrooms upstairs and two little rooms downstairs, with the kitchen added onto the back. I did a lot of work inside the house, to turn it into a home; there were bits of antique furniture in each of the rooms, and on the walls hung the pictures and paintings we had collected over the years. I dug a fishpond in the front garden, and over the front gate I made an arch, with clematis and honeysuckle. I constructed a patio where my wife and daughter could sit to sunbathe. It was heaven on earth, a dream cottage for my lovely family, with our little cat completing the picture. What more could one want?

But the beast was by now impatient of its cage and wanted out. I would look in the shop windows at all the lovely dresses and jewellery, and even bought perfume which I was afraid to wear. Barbara had two brothers and a younger sister; the odds were stacked against me being able to exercise my inner identity, and the pressure grew worse. I got caught out by my mother-in-law one evening, when I had tried out some lipstick that I'd bought and couldn't remove it. Although she obviously knew what it was, she said nothing, as if it might go away on its own.

Life became increasingly tortuous and strange feelings rose inside me. Sometimes it felt as though my skin moved over my body like some other skin, someone else's, and my stomach would feel as though I might be sick, but not unpleasantly so. The whole experience was more eerie than unpleasant, as if my other self was moving in me like a foetus in the womb, occasionally kicking. Then it would go away. These experiences were to last for many years.

My real mother began to visit more frequently, and we got to know each other better. My wife, being the more sympathetic of us, would often cook her a nice dinner, and I would collect her in the car and take her home again, the dutiful son, I suppose. By now, I had bought a small collection of female clothing which I would wear when there was no one in the house, and I took the name of Karen. One Sunday, when my mother was at the cottage, I went upstairs, put on my best dress for her and came into the room dressed as Karen. She looked up and said, 'Oh Freddy, you would have been a lovely girl!' And that is when I told her that a girl was what I wanted to be. I wished then that I had been brought up by her. She made no further comment, and it was never mentioned again, but I had needed to tell someone, and she seemed to understand.

A few weeks before Easter, I had made her a Sunday dinner of roast chicken with Martini sauce, which my wife had taught me to cook. After dinner, my mother looked up at me and said, in her quiet way, 'Lovely.' It was the first and only dinner that I cooked for her, as she died of a heart attack on Easter Sunday. The moment she died, I could feel the force of her attack and then her absence from the world. It was as though I was somewhere near, or that some part of her was inside of me. We had always, from the first frightening moment together, had a special line of communication between us. On one occasion, I felt a message from her whilst I was in Kingston on Thames, and left immediately to return to Plymouth. When I arrived on her doorstep, she calmly told me that she knew I was coming. Earlier in the year of her death, she bought me an axe for the cottage fires and said, 'When you use this axe you can remember me.' At the time of her death I was in the process of chopping wood for the fires, but with such ferocity and power that it had to be her moment of departure from this world. It was as though she cried out her goodbye to me across the void.

I broke down in deep mourning after the policeman left the house, and really felt the loss of someone I never knew properly. I undoubtedly didn't care enough, but perhaps I could never know her as others know their parents. I feel sad that I can't show her the daughter she could have had, although she was very proud of me as a son. On her wreath, I wrote the words, 'To the mother I never knew, from the son she never had.'

Chapter 14. Karen

I had long since been hunting men at night, to satisfy the hunger in me to be made love to as I wished, and I lived, during what seemed an eternity, for love in cars, parks and beds. Then there were the nights with my wife, when I would lie in bed beside her, burning with the pain of what I had done with some strange man. I felt disgusted and ashamed of myself, and the feeling grew worse every time it happened. Sex between Barbara and I grew to be the exception, engaged in only during moments of mutual need for each other, but remaining in the background, as a wall of resentment built between us, and the arguments grew more bitter.

My loneliness increased. It didn't have to be sex all the way; an embrace was often enough to make me feel as though I would melt. I felt safe and secure with men, and my body felt warm in their embrace, just as it did all those years before in the bed of my Cousin Billy. I had always found the strength and power of men's arms comforting and protective, with the hard muscles in their shoulders and neck and the beautiful shape of their chest. I wanted absolute oneness with them as I sat astride their strong bodies and felt the strength of them inside me. I wanted to see them naked, with the soft light on their skin, and to feel the hard difference of their very being, the way they dealt with the world and took from it what they wanted, master of all they saw. I wanted to see this man at my table, strong and yet vulnerable to my wishes. I don't talk of the animals that stalk the streets, but of the real men who quietly move through space and look through eyes that can read feelings and respond to them with kindness, warmth and love. This was the man that I found I could never be, and always wanted.

Arrogant and bad tempered, I trampled my way through all my women's lives, without knowing the chaos I caused. I fed from them, knowing only how to give the softness and gentleness, the kissing adoration and kind consideration that were rightfully theirs. It gave me pride of a different sort to be with a man on the street. I felt proud to be able to say to the world, 'this is *my* man' and feel his confidence and strength as he walked along beside me, unknowing of my feelings towards him. With some men, my head would swim, and I didn't want to go from them. The sick feelings increased until they became part of every day. Buying female clothing was a socially difficult exercise for so obvious a male as I was, and many an embarrassing moment with shop assistants was the reward for my brave attempts to dress properly. The driving need to dress and identify as a woman grew stronger and more compulsive, until I did so at every given opportunity. It did not enter my mind to see a doctor - I was afraid to. I was afraid of going insane, as my mother had. I lived deep inside my male shell, working alongside men and hating it, with all their comments about queers, which I now thought I was. When I wore perfume in their company, they said I smelled like a prostitute's handbag. It was horrible, and I was always glad to get away from them. Some men had such a strong effect on me that I could not be near them, and at one point I was very much in love with one of our best friends. I would have killed for him. He was warm and deep, and I had to work hard not to let my feelings show. It was an awfully painful time.

One night, I met a boy of nineteen who wanted to make love to me. He was very attractive, and I wanted badly to feel his skin next to mine and smell his body against me, to feel his lovely curves and muscles. I brought some of my clothes with me from home, and we went to his flat. I dressed for him, and he made love to me in the most exquisite manner. I was totally lost from that moment on. I wanted to be pregnant by him and it was though I could feel his sperm in me for days afterwards. I wanted so badly to have his child and to be completely accepted by him as the woman I now felt myself to be, and went into a deep depression in the knowledge that I could never have his or any other child. I knew my life was to take a new turn, and the real me had emerged.

I could not say a thing to my poor wife, and suffered five years of total confusion about my sexual state. I wasn't gay, that much I knew. I searched for ways to develop my female self, and managed to get some oestrogen birth pills from a friend of mine. I spent many evenings in the bath at the cottage, fighting with myself, but there were two of me, and the man in me was losing the battle. I thought I was on the verge of a mental breakdown, the possibility of suicide crossing my mind many times, but I could not do that to my lovely family. Apart from the wonderful feelings when I made love with a man, there hadn't initially been many manifestations of my dual sexuality, and I hadn't really known what my terrible feelings of self-hate were about. Now, I went through a period of absolute disgust at the sight of my naked body, crazily trying to permanently remove all my body hair, much to the annoyance of my dear wife. I would shave all over, ending up with a shaving rash and itching like a bag of fleas. I tried to comb my hair into a more female style and did all that I could to be as female as possible. My mood swings got progressively worse, until I was so bad that a ladder in my tights or a torn fingernail would set me off crying. I would get to such a pitch sexually that I felt as if the sperm in my body had leaked out into my blood stream and was poisoning my system. It made my arms feel heavy, and made me very depressed, until I got some form of release either through masturbation or sexual intercourse. I began to realise that, to be complete as a woman, I would have to take the same road as Cochinell all those years before. Life was unbearable. As far as I was concerned, I had not been that bad a person, but wanted to destroy myself at times. Sometimes a day would start well enough, but then there was another person in me, wanting to tell me how to run the day, or how I should feel towards someone, while my other self just wanted to be left alone, to get on with whatever I was doing. I often did things without understanding why I had done them and would sit for ages wondering why I had hurt myself or someone around me. When I thought I was going insane, my thoughts would go back to my mother, then to my father, and I would temporarily hate them both. I grew afraid of myself, and it went in circles: fear, hate, and at times a total loss of who I was and what I was doing here.

Meanwhile, I was at the peak of my expertise in cabinet making and was the best for miles around. I had gained skills and made things that others could only wonder at, and yet I could do nothing with these wonderful gifts I had been given. When I looked at the photos of my work, then considered the whole of my life, the two didn't match at all. They were two pieces from different puzzles. I drew more and more away from the world around me, into a place where nothing registered as being real. Then I did something I had wanted to do for a long time, and had my ear pierced. I wanted to have them both done, so that I could wear a pair of earrings, but I had to settle for just the one, in order that I still presented the macho image that everyone around me wanted. It was extremely frustrating, but it was the first real step towards doing something about the way I often felt about myself. When the girl in me arose, I would imagine that I could dress completely and go out into the world as me, to enjoy to the absolute full the heady feeling of feminine beauty and softness that permeated my body and mind.

The desires grew stronger by the month, and soon, against the wishes of my wife, I had the other ear pierced. I wore the merest hint of eye shadow at times, mostly at night, when the world couldn't really see it, but I grew progressively bolder, and would wear a shade of blusher in the daytime, and two earrings. It was getting more obvious to all our friends that everything was not right with me. When they asked questions, I would tell them that I felt more comfortable in makeup, as it gave me a bit of colour, but deep inside, the woman was stirring and making her presence more strongly known.

I had used the name Karen, for some time, in the gay bars, the only safe place to go in female clothing. I was well known, although not accepted by the gays, and if I wore a dress there, hardly a soul would speak to me, let alone dance with me. Once again, the two-pronged fork: I either went 'straight' and got to dance with someone, or dressed as I preferred, and got to dance with no one. I was once invited to a drag ball at a gay club, but after some periods of living full time as a woman, I sat in the auditorium with the rest of the spectators, feeling completely isolated, as I was the only other male there dressed in female attire. The men in drag wanted me to join them on the stage, as if I was one of them, but I could only feel insulted that men could parody women and dress in that fashion, with puffed out wigs and overblown dresses, so I left to go home on my own. These experiences illustrate how lonely life was becoming. To go to a club and be left alone for the whole of the evening made me want to crawl away and die. These were people I had known for so long, and now they turned their backs on me as if I was a stranger. It was another dilemma to cope with. In male clothing I could get almost anyone I wanted; I was slim, strong looking and attractive to both male and female, there was no problem. But in female clothing I got nothing but left out by both sexes, which was not what I wanted at all. I wanted my own man, someone special to whom I could give myself completely, someone to melt into and feel his love wash over me.

I hunted at night, in different clubs and bars, but found no one with whom I had an affinity, until one evening I met John. He was a very wary man, and as he had been beaten up and robbed a few times it was difficult to get close to him. He was cautious, and it was quite a long time before he took me to his house. We often made love in his car, but it was never satisfactory, although we pleased each other. One evening, he took me home and we sat for hours talking about ourselves, and generally getting to know each other better. He knew I was married, and that there was never to be anything permanent, but we felt safe with each other. No more hunting was needed. John was slim, with blonde hair, and was athletic, running a few miles every evening. He was the same age as me. We were well matched; there was no competition between us. Our wishes were the same, in as much as we both needed someone to love. That first night we went to bed together in a proper bed, he was beautiful. His muscles were long and strong and he was slender and youthful. We rode together like the waves on a beach, hour after hour; we took of each other, and gave the pleasure that we both sought, and all the time Karen came nearer to the surface. Every piercing thrust served to give her the breath of life she so eagerly and desperately needed, till the fires burned in her body, and entirely consumed my maleness. My head swam and my stomach turned over and over. My insides felt like warm oil. I sat astride him and gently rocked back and forth, bringing him to orgasm. I loved the look in his eyes when he came, and when I reached orgasm, I sank onto him to feel our sperm mix on our chests and stomachs. But it was bittersweet, the overwhelming desire to conceive leaving the taste of miserable failure.

Karen grew stronger, and as she grew, the man I had once been disintegrated, becoming a shadow-like, dilute reminder of a once virile male. As we swam in each other's sexual power, I got further and further from what was once me. Although it was never love, we gave each other machine energy. There was nothing rough about the way John made love, he stroked and kissed my body, and I did the same with his strong self. He would part my legs with the gentlest of pressure, and just the touch of his fingers inside my thighs would open me up like a flower. I have never had the desire to penetrate a man, but to feel him pushing against me would bring waves of excitement, and carry me into a dream world, where my body would melt into his and we would be as one, moving in unison. This beautiful thing with John lasted for nearly a year, but Karen wanted to come right out, and I expressed the desire for him to make love to me and treat me as a woman, and for him to let me wear a dress and love me like that. It somehow poisoned our relationship, and we drifted apart until we saw nothing more of each other - to be expected, I suppose. It was back to the hunting, but it took me a long time to find anyone who could love like my John.

Then, in 1982, AIDS hit the world. All doors closed, mine included, and the lovemaking had to stop. The guilt that I lived with, because of my unfaithfulness towards my wife, crippled me inside. I felt twisted and damaged. A part of me was bruised beyond healing. There was no way I could relay my thoughts and feelings to her or anyone at all. I was locked inside with the knowledge of what I had done to her and my daughter, and the feeling of Karen getting stronger. It was a bitter poison that I drank every day, and there was no way to escape.

Karen was out now. I thought differently, felt differently, I was different. There was almost nothing left of my former self, and the days grew long in the knowledge that I would never be the same father and husband that I once was. Very much alone in a frightening place, where the days were as dark as night, the spark had gone from me, and now there was just misery and fear in a bewildering world of not knowing how to cope. The softer side of Karen gave me warmth and comfort, but the split rent me in two. Loneliness and despair grew rapidly worse; I couldn't concentrate on my business and would earn only enough to pay the bills, certainly not enough for luxuries. We all suffered, all three of us. The house was falling apart but I couldn't escape from the prison inside of me to do anything about it. I recognised the restricting bars that had held me fast all my life. Karen grew stronger by the day, no longer in the background, with me in everything I did. We worked and lived in a strained harmony together, making compromises and imposing a certain constraint on each other.

I cried to sleep in the dark and wondered if there was any way out of this abject misery. I could not be me as a male, and I could not be me as a female, and between the two stood my lovely wife and daughter. That gave me more pain than anything else, I did not want to hurt them, and here I was killing all three of us. The arguments grew worse and worse; it was a living hell for us all.

My insistence on wearing women's clothing grew more emphatic by the day, and the strain grew proportionally worse. The visits from our one-time friends grew less and less frequent, until they stopped altogether. My dress sense was terrible, and every time I went out into the world, my wife worried that I would be mugged or beaten up. It got to a point where I would not wear men's clothing in the house at all, insisting on changing into a dress as soon as I came in. It was my new and rightful way of life, and now I had found it, I was not going to give it up. I had at last discovered myself, and now felt the urgent need to seal the knot, deciding that if I didn't do something about my physical state I would slowly go mad. At the same time the feeling of frustration grew stronger, there was still something missing inside. The sensation of my skin moving had long since gone, the feeling was now right through my body. Yet still I did not know how to make the change.

It was the occasion of my daughter's birthday, all the tables had been laid out with food, the candles were in the chandelier, as was normal at times of celebration, and everything looked wonderful for her. She had invited her favourite female friends and some of the boys from her school. They arrived in twos and threes, and soon the room was full of girls in their best dresses. They all looked extremely pretty and colourful, and the room was drenched in femininity and perfume. I managed to stand the sight of them for about half an hour before I needed to join them in a dress and feel the same as them. My daughter had known for quite some time that I cross dressed, and after some consultation with her and my wife, it was decided that I could dress as long as I made a game of it and played the servant or something. I went upstairs and put on my prettiest dress and best makeup and came down into their midst. They thought it was great, and for the whole of the afternoon I waited on them, but inside I felt as though I was one of them, I felt that I belonged. It didn't seem to alter their opinion of my daughter or me, and the episode was hardly ever mentioned again.

My wife rode on that train to hell with me. I struggled to explain to her how I felt inside, but the hurt was so great that I couldn't tell her how bad it really was. I felt destroyed, stabbed through from the front and back. On the one hand there was the fear of losing her, and on the other hand was the sure knowledge that I would. Both sides cut me deep, and the knowledge of her suffering brought me pain beyond all comprehension, yet compulsive drive led me to the birth pills I had acquired. The small number of pills I had at the house peeped at me from their hiding place, most were kept far away, at my workshop, my wife having threatened to destroy anything she found. I knew they were the Pandora's box to my body's development; I also knew that once I had started to take them, there would be no turning back. Every day that went by brought me closer to the final moment of capitulation, and eventually Karen won. I took the first pill on the prescribed start day of the pack and continued through the month. I then started on the second pack. The guilt I felt about my wife was torture, and the time had come to tell her that I was taking the pills, was seriously crippled inside as a man, could no longer function as one, and wanted to live as a woman. It was devastating for us both. She begged me to stop taking the pills and see a doctor, but I was now afraid of losing my identity, and refused to see anyone. I felt that I was on the verge of a new journey into femininity - the door to my womanhood from the physical side; mentally I was already well on the way. At last I had the key to some other part of me.

Within a fortnight or so my mood swings quietened, I felt softer in myself and less harassed. I was afraid though; I knew there was no way back. But there was another worry: what would happen when the pills ran out? By now, my wife knew the situation and was as deep in the shock of it as myself. Again, she begged me to go and see a doctor. I was frightened to death; I didn't know what they would say at the surgery. I went to the doctor's only to find that my own GP was away, replaced temporarily by a woman. I don't know how I told her that I wanted to be a woman, that I was trapped in the wrong body. She made me an appointment with the local psychiatrist, and the two weeks wait were like two years. I knew I couldn't go on for a lot longer without some form of treatment and was almost ill with the worry of trying to keep alive and refrain from killing myself.

The visit to the psychiatrist was one of the worst moments of all. I explained my dilemma and was terrified of what would happen to me, fully expecting to be committed to a mental hospital like my mother had been; certain that the curse that had awaited me from childhood was finally upon me. Instead, I was prescribed the appropriate medicine. My fear diminished, but this was short-lived as the reality of a broader female identity dawned.

By now, the atmosphere in the house was unbearable for everyone; I already insisted on dressing as a woman in the house all the time, and for the previous two or three years had gone out at night dressed as Karen. My wife was worried sick, for herself, for my daughter, and for me. The situation was intolerable by any standards. I knew that if I didn't go from the house for good, I would slowly kill us all. No one came to visit any more. With our friends gone, it left us with ourselves; in their ignorance, it was the worst thing they could have done. Support was what we needed, rather than friends and relatives failing to understand

and rejecting us, as so often seems to be the way. My birthday was due. My wife normally put on lavish celebrations, but this year would be different. No party, only sadness stalked the house, and two days later I left the home I had helped to create and destroy.

The door back was now firmly closed, and there remained only my future life. I changed my name from Karen, finding Joy a softer, lovelier name, reflecting the new softness I felt. I now knew who I was and had been prescribed the necessary oestrogen. On the fourth of July, I had my first consultation in London, and my first prescription for the female hormone, Premarin. On reflection, this day was my independence day, and I felt that, for the first time, life said 'Yes!' releasing me from the power that had held me for so long, to live a life without the pain and torture I had suffered for so many years, through so many events.

I changed my documentation with my solicitor and came away with tears in my eyes, overwhelmed by the emotion of the day. From that moment, I was legally a woman, and my name was legally Joy, the wonderful feeling reinforced by the solicitor saying, 'I wish you the best of luck for the future, Joy.' I was at last recognised by authority as a woman and ventured forth to fulfil my new role in society. Despite what had happened in the family, I was extremely proud to have at last reached this point in a life that had haunted me for so long.

Chapter 15. Transition

I lived with a friend for about six weeks, during which time I came more and more to terms with my new identity and took to going out in the daytime, dressed as Joy. It took a lot of nerve, but I had plenty of that. I must have looked an awful sight in those first few months of public exposure. I did not have the most wonderful head of hair and had no money to buy myself a decent wig, the wearing of which, anyway, I considered to be a transvestite trait, and fought against.

The men I met on the street were, in the main, foul-mouthed creatures, and I sometimes wondered if I wanted to be with a man at all. They made disgusting comments, and I felt great pity for their wives and girlfriends, somewhere at home perhaps, left to take care of the chores and struggle with motherhood, while their men, unbeknown to them, were throwing sexual innuendoes at other women on the streets. A lot of filthy abuse came my way, par for the course for many transsexuals, as they continued to be whipping posts for society. Women, I found, were largely quite understanding, whereas these men were almost exclusively ignorant of the finer feelings of human suffering and tragedy. It seemed to me that men followed their instincts while women followed their intellect, but this didn't entirely undermine my instinctive need to be half of a biological pair with a male. I grew a thick, hard shell to protect myself against the comments, and felt sad to think that they might treat natural born women in the same way, seeing only the dirty side of love between the sexes. It was impossible to reason with them at all, and these encounters left me wounded.

It became very dangerous for me to walk late at night. I didn't go into pubs or clubs alone and developed a sixth sense about the people who walked on the streets alongside me. During the day, I tried to carry on in my trade as a cabinet maker, and early in the evening, I would walk miles and for many hours to avoid having to sit alone. I left my friend's house and moved into a small bedsit, desperate to find my own place in society and to live my life at last in a normal way, to somehow start all over again, rightfully, as a woman. Loneliness is a knife with the sharpest edges; it cuts at all times and from all angles. My room had no memory of my wife and daughter in it. There were none of the familiar things or smells. I don't know how I kept alive for the first few weeks in that place. I didn't know how to cook until, after eight or nine weeks, my daughter wrote some simple recipes that kept me in good health, and although I tried to keep as clean as possible, as I hated to be even the slightest bit dirty, there were no facilities to wash my clothing. I was on such a high dose of the female hormone that I could smell it in my sweat, sweet and warm, like mother's milk. It was very comforting, and almost my only companion. This smell of my femininity kept me warm at night and held the ghosts at bay. I couldn't bear to think of my wife and daughter at the cottage alone, vulnerable to all that was bad in the world. Life seems to sniff out its victims, and bring the wolves to their doors, and so it was with my family. I cried myself to sleep every night, and well into the day. There were times when I would stand in the workshop and cry, and I worked automatically, like a robot. The pain was terrible, and I thought there was no way I could continue under this strain for a lot longer. I could not kill myself, because I loved my family so, and I could not stay alive with the pain that ripped me from the inside. For five months, no-one came near; my world seemed to shrink to within a few feet of me, so there was only the minute I was in. I seemed to run completely out of tomorrows.

It was then that I made contact with the only people who could really understand, instigated by the Gender Identity Clinic at Charing Cross Hospital, with whom I had been put in touch by my own GP in Plymouth, some few weeks after our first consultation. They were a Plymouth based self-help group of transsexuals, that came to me in my hour of greatest need. I was at the end of my tether and they brought light into my dark, cavernous world.

I once spent the weekend at the house of a transvestite I met in the town. It was strange to see a man dressed in female clothing, when he still looked like a man, and disconcerting to know that here was a man, but you couldn't see the outline of his body and the male strength that normally showed. It was the first time that I could see what my wife had seen when I used to dress in the early days, before I feminised and wore makeup properly. I suddenly felt her pain as I tried to come to terms with his appearance and to relate to the real person I knew lay underneath the veneer of his dress. I knew that I could never live with or love a man that wore female clothing and could not relate to this chameleon. It was as though there was a double person standing there, a twin-sexed person with no name or solidity, a double image in one shell, and I saw the fading image of myself as I once had been, a dim reflection in a dusty mirror looking back at me from some other time. I felt the emptiness that my wife must have felt when she realised that the image she knew was too far away to touch. Each of us floated on ice flows, with dark waters between us, getting further apart all the while. Reaching out across the water to grip the hand of the loved one, the gap was too great, so wide that it was possible only to shout of love and helplessness to the other across the void.

Every transsexual person has his or her own uncharted wilderness to travel through. Although the loneliness and pain are the same, the landscapes are different. We must learn to live with the subconscious building blocks that make up each individual. Being confronted with yourself, as though in a mirror, is painful, as we live with a picture of our own image as projected to the world, wearing it like a piece of clothing. This becomes so familiar that it *seems* to be the individual. But is it necessarily the real person? When you come to see the real you, the mirror cracks and there is something behind the mirror that you never realised was there. Suddenly, there is all that life has made you - not necessarily the thing you wanted. I don't believe that anyone could want to go through transition for the exercise; it is a nightmare of self-truths that only the strongest can survive. There is guilt, and not knowing whether you are right to feel things, where the feelings come and why they come. Questions such as: who makes you what you are and what powers and influences make you the person you find yourself to be, rush at you in the quietest moments of the night or the busiest times of the day. You question every action and emotion you have experienced, investigate the depth of your being and your family history. There comes an urgency to find answers. No more blithely going from day to day, this becomes a fight for mental survival, a storm that never abates.

As the pain of the storm grew ever deeper, I thrashed around for a way to go back to my family and be the me I had once known. But there was no way back from this wild, stormy, moorland place, where the wind tore through my bones and I was left totally naked. I was long on that path in that wilderness. With the help of the hormones, and a better grasp of myself, I gradually felt better inside, but the feelings of guilt towards my family remained as sharp as ever. I eventually wrote to my wife in an effort to explain why I could never again return home to her. It was something we both wanted, for this nightmare to end, and for me to re-join the family, but that was no longer possible. In the world I was now in, there was only one way, and that was forward. It was as though the path behind me disappeared when I turned to go back. It was like standing at the edge of a cliff.

My wife and I started to communicate via the occasional letter, and she began to understand that I hadn't wanted to hurt her in the things I did, but that this was my destiny, and Joy was here to stay. My breasts began to develop, my features softened, and my hair grew very fine. I became more wary of men, and my sexual feelings began to diminish, to the extent that I no longer desired women in any way and felt an even greater kinship with them than I did before. Sometimes I could feel the male sexual side of me, somewhere in the shadows, like a ghost receding by the day. It's a strange experience to watch your sexuality fade, not unlike losing a limb, there is a ghost left in its place for some time after. At times, I would see girls on the street and think to myself how lovely they looked and how nice it might be to make love to them. My mind and body would send the appropriate messages to various parts of me, to prepare for the encounter that may ensue. But the messages would stop above the waistline, as my erogenous zones focused on other parts of my body, so the feeling of desire would linger, find no resting place, and fade away. Gradually, this became a more external experience, as though I could feel my maleness standing a short distance away from me. The messages that were sent from my brain to my nether regions were projected to the figure that stood beside me, and dissolved there instead of returning to me as a negative response. I saw the reason for having to live in the female role for a minimum of one year before surgery: the physical aspects and mental attitude must be completely changed in order to avoid damage to the delicate body and mind that nature has created for us to live in. I rowed my little boat on the sea of torture, battling storms of mental anguish and perpetual torment, to stand on the shores of the other world. I now looked forward to fulfilling my wish to be with the man I would choose to be my partner for the rest of my life. It had been a hard and tiring journey, and although it was not yet over, I felt that the worst was behind me.

The feelings of guilt were now almost gone, and I was learning to put aside any sadness I felt towards my situation. I had a new life to embark upon, and the ghosts from my past were gradually lying down. I often wonder how much of our lives are predetermined. I think about sitting at my sister's dressing table, as a little boy, removing durex from their tiny packets and slipping them over my fingers, and tying a sanitary towel around my face. When my sister Jane caught me, I explained that I was going to be a surgeon. And what about all the literature I read about gynaecology, or the dresses that I wore as a child, or the lovely feeling I experienced in the company of my sister and all the other females over the years? Were they indicators of what was to come? I have wondered, of all the people in the world, why me? I have considered all I did to take on female attributes: having a woman anoint my inner thighs with her sex scent, harbouring the secret wish for the scent to be from my own body, at other times requesting that women urinate on my stomach or between my legs, as a substitute for a man's ejaculation. At times, I was intensely jealous of the woman under me during sex and wished I was her and that this wonderful strong man was making love to me; I would manoeuvre the situation in order to be the one physically underneath, experiencing the warmth and closeness of another person on top of me as though I was a girl.

My breasts and skin surface became more sensitive, over time, and when I was with a man, I could feel the centre of the short muscular area between the rear of my penis and my anal opening becoming hot and wanting penetration. I knew that was impossible, and this frustrated me. Sometimes my whole genital area would ache for the penetration that would bring my man and I together in a oneness of being. The experiences I had with the male monsters on the street when I first came out began to fade in intensity, and I could at last walk in public and feel no embarrassment at meeting other people, the ridicule and offensive remarks becoming less frequent.

I felt more confident, and as the months rolled by the feeling of social inferiority began to fade. I was becoming more accepted as the woman I wanted to be. It was no longer a painful ordeal to go about a daily routine. I still had the workshop, and dealt with my customers in the same way as I had always done, but there was understandably a strained feeling between us as though they thought I had gone insane. In addition, my workmates felt they were dealing with two people, and this caused a lot of stress. It came to the point that if I didn't leave the cocoon of their company, I would never be able to deal with the rest of society in my new gender role. I sold the business and enrolled on a training course in fashion and dressmaking. I was faced with about twenty women, all natural born and most of them mothers. It was a lovely safe feeling, like being back in the womb. It was warm, whereas in the world of men it had been cold and hard. I could feel the security of motherhood all around me. There was no strain here, and as I have an outgoing nature, I got on well with everyone. It might have been different in a factory environment, but I would have accepted that as well, rather than continue trying to establish my identity in the world of men, as I had tried to do in my workshop.

Identifying with the women around me came easily and I became very close to the girl who taught me. It was a frightening feeling to be so close to another female, and it concerned me for months that, as I sat close to her, I would reach out and somehow make love to her. What I felt was not sexual, but I began to worry that my maleness was returning and that perhaps those feelings towards women had not gone away. I felt like an armless amputee, with ghosts of arms wanting to embrace another entity that was often close enough to touch, yet with a wall of glass between us through which words could pass, whilst feelings stayed on the side of friendship. There could be no erotic feelings anymore, that was gone for the time being, but for how long, only the surgeon could know. I eventually talked with one of the girls, and she reassured me that it was not a sexual feeling, but a bond of friendship between the two of us. She said that women often experience it and that there were no elements of lesbianism. This reassured me that I was not experiencing male feelings at all, but the sisterly love that some women have towards others. It also served to reinforce my belief in myself and my development towards true womanhood. I had never had such a bond as a man towards another man; it was utterly alien to me. I never knew what it was to have a mate, as other men do; I always seemed to fall for men as potential lovers. My problem with males was compounded by the fact that I never felt able to express my deeper feelings for them because of social taboos.

To my new women friends, I expressed the opinion that my sister bonds with perhaps one female out of a hundred would each give me one piece of hundreds that make up my true identity. As a man, it had been necessary to clothe myself in male armour and take up weapons to protect my soft inner self - I could in no way allow myself to be vulnerable to the piercing glances of my male counterparts. Because of this armour and being aware, for every waking moment, of my vulnerability, I was left no opportunity to identify with my real self beneath the image I had to project. But now I no longer had to clothe myself in imagery and enact a part for the world, I had time to discover elements of my true self as a woman, in the many other women around me. The women I identified with would give me pieces of the puzzle which I could lay down and recognise as the woman I am. We talked of being lost in the immense transsexual wilderness, with no paths, maps or rules. Occasionally, though, a guide appears, in the form of a piece of identity, and shows the way towards the outer edge of the wilderness. We talked about sex, and the difference between someone fucking your body or making love to you - the 'someone' who makes love, so your body melts, and the 'someone else' who fucks your body and is cold. We were able to identify in the same way and express a preference for that heated lovemaking.

'When I sit and talk with you, I know I am sitting and talking with a woman and feel I am able to talk about anything,' said my new friend. I told her that between myself and my transsexual friends there was not this natural sister bond, because they were in a whirl as I was, where it is not an instinctive part of our original make up. That is why I particularly value the sister bond between myself and a natural born woman.

At some point earlier that year, I thought that, in the absence of a man to love me as a woman, I would find a lesbian girl with whom I could have the warmth of human contact I had desperately sought in the past. But as I thought about the progression of the idea of sleeping with a woman, my ardour diminished when it came to the point of lovemaking, with the possibility of her penetration of my body an empty wish. It was a cold reality that a woman could never be the lover that I sought, and I got used to the idea that there was never to be a woman in my life in that way again. It was a strange thought, as I remembered all the men I had slept with, and thought that could be construed as homosexuality, in the same way as if I now slept with another woman. Would I be considered homosexual if, with a male body, I slept with a male as a woman? I did at one point find a man to sleep with. It was a frustrating experience, where I had a man who wanted to make love to me, but though we made love of sorts, there was the ultimate frustration of his inability to pierce me where it ached the most. I could have cried for both of us, knowing we could not unite, that I could not give him the true satisfaction that he wanted, and could not be fully the woman that I felt myself to be. Although the experience left me thinking life was unjust, I also realised that in a short few months I would not be far from the ultimate fulfilment of my life's ambition, and that soon I may undergo the surgery I wanted and needed.

During this first year of transition, my body took on a more rounded appearance, my facial skin softened, and the hair growth that had been so strong on my arms and chest weakened and lost its ginger colour, becoming almost transparent and very fine in texture. My legs lost their defined muscularity and became more shapely. My stomach rounded, so I believed I was getting fat and embarked on a series of exercises to trim my waist. It paid off, and I was able to control the layers of fatty tissue that wanted to form around my midriff, although that still left the problem of cellulite on my thighs. My once strong, muscular arms, that had pushed so much weight in the gymnasium during my youth, now gave way to slenderness. But, although my fingers appeared more slender, my hands remained large and strong. I had long learned to walk in a graceful manner, moving from the hip, and felt the graceful movement flow through my body as I walked along the street, my breasts moving in sympathy with the rest of me. They had, in the course of some eight months, grown to overfill a hand, my body measuring thirty-eight inches at the bust, twenty-eight inches at the waist, and thirty-eight inches at the hips. The proportions were perfect. My hair, which had long languished under a wig, now reached my shoulders. It was a bit fine but looked a lot better that it had done earlier in the year.

I had, in this short time, eaten twenty-five thousand, seven hundred milligrams of Androcur and two thousand, two hundred milligrams of Premarin. Androcur is an anti-androgen drug, which blocks the action of male sex hormones and diminishes the male sex drive. It helps to protect against baldness of the scalp and lessens the strength of the hair growth on those parts of the body that the male sex hormone, testosterone, affects. It also causes atrophy of the prostate gland and the testicles and eventually leads to sterilisation in the male. Other side effects are the slow growth of male breasts into the tiny buds seen in juvenile girls, a general quietening of mood, and the suppression of ego. I had for some months been unable to ejaculate, and when my sex drive arose, it came from somewhere deeper than it had as a man, when it had always been evident on the surface. Now, it was quiet and deep moving, slow to react to outside stimulus, although when fully aroused was far more powerful and longer lasting than before. When orgasm was finally reached, the waves of trembling could last for anything up to half an hour after the last orgasmic peak. These effects were due to the combined action of the Androcur and high doses of oestrogen, in the form of Premarin, which is made from the urine of pregnant mares. It is responsible for the general softening of body contours, and changes in the brain and thought patterns, with the resultant stress that is part of transsexualism. The drug Premarin also enlarges the breasts, narrows the waist and fattens the hips, changing the male shape beyond recognition. There is no drug yet, however, that can alter the voice, and therapy must be undergone to achieve this. I lived in hope that I disguised my voice sufficiently to pass in conversation in public without sounding out of place. My facial hair was gradually removed by electrolysis, an expensive process that can take two to three years, and in the more stubborn cases, even longer, although the oestrogen and Androcur combination go a long way to weakening the growth. Facial features change with the prolonged use of the drugs, and the point arrives when even relatives and family may barely recognise the individual.

Chapter 16. Setting Sail

I met two other trans women and we became a family; no one else could better understand our particular pain. We were totally self-supporting and available to each other in times of distress, and at any other given time. On many occasions, I was more than glad to have that support and comfort. It sometimes felt that to continue was beyond strength and reason and that a better way would be the exhaust pipe or the razor. I suppose the knowledge that the remnants of my original family were still out there somewhere, along with the family to which I now belonged, stopped any bid to end it all. I knew what pain it would bring to the others in the group who somehow had the strength to carry on. My daughter regularly visited the tiny flat that I had made my home, and I used some of the recipes remembered from my wife, to cook for her. Barbara was now becoming a more distant, less familiar figure to me, but on our rare meeting, the shock of her image still reverberated through my body and shook me for many hours afterwards. She was like a drug to me, and I found it extremely difficult not to visit her at the tiny cottage that had been our home for so long. It was strange to see her forming a new life and slowly becoming someone I didn't know anymore. I stood by, in case she needed the limited protection and help I could now afford. The man and wife were gone; we were now sisters, and I saw her as a woman who'd had a terrible time of it over seventeen years. I still loved her deeply, and stayed in the background of her life, watching her grow more confident, a slow and difficult process.

Having been a man in a man's world gave me the slight edge and at times was a distinct advantage. It was amusing to see males in their act to impress and woo women. Some of the approaches that they made were quite funny, and some downright stupid, but I was always instinctively wary and considered what their real motives were in wanting to know me. Males really did seem to be a different species to women; if it wasn't enough to feel different from them all through my life, it now became a direct observation as I grew ever more apart. They had a confidence that women could, until recently, only look at from another room. This was a world built and run by men. They claimed to have created virtually everything in it and sat with the confidence of gods over their creation. Nothing much seemed to shake them, but when it did, they reacted as if their world had been taken away from them. In most males I saw only large grown children, mostly spoiled by their parents, and more affected by experiences in their youth than females. I found that women were generally better able to cope with the rough ride that life sometimes brought, seeming, in the main, more resilient and stronger mentally than the males around them. It is fair to say, though, that there were also some very gentle male beings in my circle, some of whom had suffered deeply in their lives and just wanted peace.

I learned that living in pain brings humility and sensitivity not formerly possessed, and that was one of the loveliest aspects of the whole experience. To be able to feel, share and understand another's suffering was, for me, a major breakthrough and slowed me down considerably in my judgement of others. I like to think I became more democratic in my way of thinking and less dogmatic in my beliefs: beliefs that I had held for many years and that had tainted my vision of the world, much to my wife's annoyance. She would often say I was insensitive to her needs and everyone else's. Now I was able to see the world as it looked through her eyes, but this character transformation had cost dear. Change such as I had gone through often brings a reversal of character. In my case, I had not previously been able to understand the stresses active inside me for all those years, and the everyday struggle was overwhelming. The battle to control my restless animal, without knowing what it was, had affected everything, and at times I felt as though I had only one arm, or half a brain to think with, or lived in half a world. The other half was like some cruel joke being enacted at my expense, and between the two halves there was always a glass wall through which I could almost see the other image of myself, yet not clearly enough to get a proper picture. I was the print of two half negatives. To have to deal with this and try to take on board another person's feelings was more than impossible, and I would storm out of the house to avoid another misunderstanding. Now the situation has changed, and I am able to accept that other half as part of me. I am at last a whole human being. But as I see the world through the eyes of a woman, I can also see better the pain that I brought my lovely wife. I only hope that I never have to live through the hell I subjected her to, which was a different hell to my own. This fear served to strengthen my defences against harmful men and to warn me of the ones who may hurt me in the same way as I did her.

It was time to see my psychiatrist in London, for what was hopefully the last consultation, and I felt that the long ride to London that day was maybe the start of yet another stage on the journey to physical womanhood, a step further in the direction of the operating table. I enquired about referral to a urologist, and my psychiatrist said he would refer me for the necessary medical examination. It was as though someone had lowered the castle drawbridge, so I was able to leave the castle and walk in the garden if I wished. There was still the main wall to pass through before the process would be at an end, physically at least. It was now time to consider what I had built around me and to take in the reality of the option now available. It wasn't a right or wrong decision but a time to consider what to do once the whole thing was over. So long as I lived in this secure castle that no other could enter, I was safe from some of the influences of the outside world. As I couldn't go to a dance and take someone home for the night, or enter into a serious affair very easily, the distance between myself and these possibilities served as a defence. The prospect of surgery took away this security and left me wide open to the world, like any other woman. On the journey home, I considered what my future course was to be, wherever I might be in the world. The prospect of returning to Germany entered my mind as a real possibility, but this would bring difficulties, such as the need to have the qualifications required to work there and earn a decent living. It was also possible that Germany would not accept my changed status and that I may have to retake my driving test to get a license. Although these were all suppositions, they were nevertheless real considerations. However, I was at the halfway point in this long journey, and I hoped it wouldn't be too long before I had my letter from the surgeon. That would leave just one more hurdle, the money to pay for the treatment, which, in 1989, was to cost me two thousand, six hundred and fifty pounds.

My course work at the college gradually improved and became more interesting under the watchful eye of my wonderful Finnish teacher, and my confidence grew by the week. I had made a few dresses and skirts, and a lovely chintz blouse for myself, and the possibility of more complicated work was on the horizon as we broke into the realm of block and pattern making. I could now use the skills learned in furniture design to further my abilities in dressmaking, and my ability to draw would allow me greater freedom in the design of clothing.

The future was as exciting as it was obscure, and through my window on the world shone the bright light of hope and a feeling of security and comfort. My being was now consolidated into a homogeneous whole; all it needed was the final polish. At first, I found it difficult to accept how well I was. I felt as though I had suffered from the flu all my life, and now I no longer had the flu my mental confusion had diminished, and it was as if I had just read all of the rules and understood the game. Able to think clearly, in a logical and precise way, something I had been unable to do for as long as I could remember, was like being born again with none of the ideas and prejudices accumulated on life's journey. After a cleansing of spirit and soul by fire, here was a new life, and the sun shone on my horizon.

A lot of my peace came from long weekends spent with my friend Hilary: weekends where I needed to do nothing but take stock of myself, and we exchanged ideas about our respective emotional states, analysing them at length, obtaining a clearer view of who and what each of us were, and where we were on the spectrum of being. There is a line of development on this journey, which seems to go roughly through three stages. The first stage is deep shock and trauma that can last for many years. Then comes a stage of acceptance of oneself and the situation. The final stage is where neurosis may cause the individual to become irrational about his or her condition. These stages can occur at different points along the path of each individual, depending on the ability of the person to cope with factors that can affect progress, such as changing emotions, social standing, whether in a relationship or single, whether or not children are involved, and so on. The second stage is the crucial point, where one becomes physically and mentally ready, and I believe that surgery should take place at this point of peak readiness. Once this peak has passed, the chances of surgery may become more remote because of the unstable nature of the individual, and thoughts of suicide, once forgotten, may become real again: surgery should not be delayed any longer than necessary.

On December 6, 1988, my wife's birthday, I moved away from the abject loneliness of the bedsit where I had run in desperation, to a tiny flat close to where my wife and daughter lived. Suddenly, ghosts and memories of our first meeting, and part of our subsequent life together, were all around me. In the next street was the flat where we had first met, and from where my first wife had disappeared. In the back garden was the orange blossom I had picked for each of my wives in turn. Here was the tiny shop where we once bought our tobacco and bread, and the small things that make up everyday living. On some mornings, the same sun shone on the same stonework of the hospital, in the same old red way. The move was the worst possible mistake, threatening any progress I made in my new life.

I took the decision to move into a house with Hilary and Mary, the two friends in the same situation as my own, to start a new life away from the streets and shadows I knew so well. Hilary was the area representative for the Gender Dysphoria Trust in Plymouth and the South West, and Mary was another lost soul in the great wilderness. We were there to comfort each other in times of distress, and the distress grew less with each week spent together. Through everything, my daughter stood on the sideline, advising me, in her quiet way, how to go about a new relationship with my wife, who I still loved. There were other women too, who were natural born and a great pleasure to be with, giving me strength and an insight into myself that I would not otherwise have had, and guiding me to my real self. Soon, I was able to read the signposts in a maze of femininity. Some of these girls became very close and allowed me to enter their world, as even though I felt myself to be a woman, there were things I could not possibly know without being shown. Parallels emerged, my female identity grew stronger, and the picture of myself grew clearer. This world tries to destroy our self-confidence and attempts to insult us, but now it failed miserably. As the new third sex we became invulnerable. We recognised the power of our femininity, learning from each other to walk tall, hold our heads high and be proud of our status as women in society. This is a pride I never felt as a man, in forty-four years.

Chapter 17. New Horizons

About a month after the visit to my psychiatrist, a letter from Hove arrived in the post. The urologist who was to perform the operation invited me to visit him on Monday, April 3, 1989, at two o'clock in the afternoon. Hilary had her referral through for the same date, so we took Mary along with us for the trip, to give us moral support on this momentous occasion. We arrived at the private consulting rooms early that afternoon and sat in nervous anticipation. Hilary and I were to have a medical examination of our genital region, and the necessary blood test to ascertain our group for the two pints of blood needed during the operation. We also had to undergo a plasma test and an AIDS test. The secretary beckoned me into the consulting room and there behind the desk sat the eminent man himself. He was the final judge on the long journey to physical womanhood. After some general questions and the physical examination, we sat and talked for a few minutes more, and then he asked, 'When would you like to come in?' All at once, the room seemed very quiet and large, and from somewhere far away, there came my own voice: 'As soon as possible, please.'

Then there was the realisation of what I had just done. All I had read about the operation came surging into my brain, and shock rolled over me. I realised I was now on the slide, and there was no way to stop the process of movement towards the operating table. It was macabre, in a way: the implications of all that lay before me, the enormity of what I had just done, the thought that life had finally brought me to a new beginning. It must be what all transsexuals feel initially, although it is not written about or mentioned, and it may be that it is such a deep private thing that it never reaches the surface.

We drove back to Plymouth in silence. Hilary's emotions so overcame her as we passed through Sussex, where she had spent much of her childhood, that she slept most of the way. It was a journey punctuated with tears of grief, relief, and the joy that beckoned like a bright light. On our return, after the emotional power of the day, we fell into our respective beds and slept a fitful sleep.

There was a wait of twelve weeks for the operation, and the shock of the prospect lasted many days. Although I was afraid, it was, on reflection, only a fear of the absolute unknown, as each of us who take this route are on our own journey to that far shore of gender reassignment, towards which I still struggled in my little boat. There was no more fantasising about another life; the reality grew daily, as my hormone intake had to be decreased to nothing two months before surgery, to reduce the possibility of thrombosis and limit risk to life. The number of tablets grew less and less, the days got fewer, the emotions were strong and mixed, the life lived pre-op was fading into obscurity and life on the other shore was about to begin.

As the days passed, I felt better. Sometimes, the reality of what was in front of me would loom up and frighten me, but the strength of Mary and Hilary, in our quiet moments, brought some measure of peace, and fears for the future gave way to thanks for the possibility of at last being able to live as I believe was intended. My emotions ranged from curiosity to fright. One hears so many stories from other trans people, that it all becomes very mystifying and sometimes the central point of the experience is lost completely. Interspersed with these feelings came the sense of some missing link with motherhood. Sometimes, the sight of little babies in their mothers' arms, all warm and cuddly, made me feel quite ill, reminding me that I would never feel that new life growing in my belly, and that my new breasts would never succour an infant. I remembered the comfort my mother gained from the dogs and cats she so loved, maternal instinct flooding through her. I would lie on the electrologist's couch and as she began the sometimes painful job of removing the hairs from my face, would feel sick and afraid as I imagined lying on a hospital trolley in readiness to go to theatre for my operation. The oddest feeling was a result of cutting down my dose of oestrogen tablets. As I reached the end of my bodily reserves, the ghost of my former maleness crept in around the edges of my femininity like another person, an unwanted force. I started to act in the strangest of ways: the old aggression came into view, bad temper hovered on the horizon, irritability niggled and gnawed, threatening to undermine the peace of mind I had come to accept as part of my new self. I was desperate to get the whole thing over with in order not to have those horrible male feelings again. Testosterone seeping in, even in minute quantities, was like being injected with cold grey lead. I felt it in my veins. I would have been happy for the surgeon to have done his work on the hospital floor or anywhere else that would accommodate me. My main priority was to have that male factory removed from my body, in order to give me back the peace that I had enjoyed for the past year, for the first time in my life.

My birthday occurred during those weeks of waiting - so very different from the year before. This time I had the company of my beloved and treasured wife and daughter. We had somehow, through all the pain and suffering, managed to form some kind of relationship, however fragile. I spent two days preparing the meal, which was also to serve as a farewell dinner for Hilary, who was to go into hospital for her operation the following weekend. We all made something of the evening, although I could sense that Hilary was missing the family that had once been hers, and towards the end of the evening she left to go up to her own little flat and have a weep at her immense losses. I knew how confused and frightened she must have felt to have that inevitable journey ahead of her, alone.

I had the urge to clear my memory of all the faces that haunted me, such as those of my mother and all my aunties and uncles and especially my former self. I don't know how it started, but desperation engulfed me. There were to be no more memories of my long-hidden past, no more questions as to who or what I was, from where I had come, or what had made me like this. It was enough now to be that wonderful thing called woman. I took every photograph and document that carried any likeness of my former self into the garden, poured a bottle of nail polish remover over them all, and set them alight. There, turning slowly through the flames, were pictures of my mother in various poses smiling up at me, then darkening with all the other ashes of the past, to blow in the breeze and catch in spider webs decorating windows of the home created by Mary, Hilary and myself. The smell of the funeral pyre filled the house for some days and clung to every surface, reluctant to leave me. There was a sense of relief, a relaxation in my soul, and I hoped that now the ghosts were laid there would be no more hauntings. I did keep one picture of my mother though, the mother I had known and not some stranger who had figured somewhere in a past life. It gives me no pain to see her smiling back, because it is a smile that I am familiar with and know very well.

During this period of waiting, I went to visit my Aunt Ann, who had been so kind to me in my early years, and Aunt Edie, who had lived at the top of lots of stairs many years before, old now, and alone, white of skin from lack of contact with the sun. I learned that she had given birth to a daughter who had died after three days. Little dolls were arranged around my aunt's bedroom and on the bed, and beside the bed stood a little cot with a dolly in it, fast asleep. The bed was laid out with fresh clean clothes for her dolly children to wear. I saw all the loneliness and sense of loss that she experienced, as had my own mother, and thought it might be better never to have had children at all than to spend life in this sad, empty way, although my aunt no doubt felt some kind of reciprocal love from the dolls' quiet faces, which always seem to smile. It was a strange sight, and I left her frail, thin self with the promise that I would see her again soon, in the company of my daughter.

My Aunt Ann told me I had always wanted to be a girl, long before I can remember expressing it, that I had always been the pretty one and she believed I should have been born a girl. I must have looked like one when I was very small, although pictures tell a different story to my eyes. Maybe I don't see myself as she saw me then, but it must have been apparent from an early age that I wasn't destined to be the man I seemed to become. I can remember from about the age of six or seven that I was different from all the other boys, although I didn't know what that difference was at the time. I only knew I had an affinity with the girls I encountered. It's strange that every one of the closest family members I have managed to talk to admit there was always something different about me. It takes a lot to come to terms with the truth after so many years of being misled by life's forces and tides that carry us through different stages and experiences. I have said, like many other transsexuals, that had I known earlier in my life, I would have done something about it; but nothing can be done until a maturity of being and spirit is reached, and one is ready. That doesn't take away the sense of loss of the life I could have had, but at least I can be happy in the thought that I can have some of that life. There are many who will never reach that point, ending their lives in frustrated misery.

Mary is a lovely woman, and our relationship grew into a form of love I had never known with anyone else. Although quiet and placid, the ghosts of her past would trouble her deeply at times. Then it was time for Hilary and me to comfort her, take her in our arms and show her the deep love and affection that we who know this journey can give each other. We alone could walk into each other's storm and pacify the restless spirit, torn and troubled by bewildering pain. She was strong of heart most of the time though; her eyes were bright and her hair a lovely brown colour. We worked together as a team, shared all household costs, and lived reasonably well. I often asked myself if I needed anything more than good company and loving spirit. In these moments, the physical side of sex with a male paled into insignificance, and I wondered if I needed a man at all. The prospect of that first encounter intrigued me, but I felt that if I had one man, it might in fact be enough after that just to be a woman. That was the experience of some transgender people, and others had taken on a lesbian relationship in preference to a heterosexual one. Transgender people are no different from the average person in the street. The fact that we are driven by our need to live as a member of the opposite sex is neither here nor there.

With Hilary away on her journey, Mary and I were left with only the other's company, and it was a time of testing how strong our love was. The element of dependence on each other was removed, as we each found our respective places in the relationship we had formed. There was no third person adding stability, no distraction to blur the view, no vibration to upset the balance between us, and the love we had found seemed strong enough, so it was with a deep satisfaction that we lay naked and happy together in the hot sun.

Awareness of our sister's journey kept us ever vigilant and ready to respond to the first cries of help from Hilary across the distance that temporarily separated us. Each day brought me closer to that which Hilary now experienced, and I felt the emptiness of her first night alone in a guest house in Brighton. It was as if I cried with her in that lonely room, with only her toy seal to keep her company. I know the whole thing affected Mary in the same way, and at times she was close to tears as her thoughts wended their way to Hilary. On the day after Hilary's departure, after our day's work, there was no face at the window to greet us, no friendly cup of tea, just silence and emptiness.

The three of us had agreed that we would not talk in any detail about our operations, but curiosity took over and by the time it came to mine, I knew about as much as I would need to. I suppose forewarned is forearmed. As the weeks passed, on her return from hospital, Hilary, with our help, good cooking and many pots of honey, gained strength and made a wonderful recovery. Now there were only a few days left before I was to make my journey.

It is strange to follow in someone's footsteps, feeling the same, knowing the same room and distances await you, and that you will go through the same process, with the same result. It does not make you any stronger, and is disturbing, but a certain numbness takes over and blocks out the whole truth. The thoughts of what will happen afterwards become unimportant, as though you know that whatever made us and brought us here will somehow cushion the blow and justify, at some point, that which has happened. The whole journey is a lonely one, from start to finish. You live with what is inside, and learn to cope with change, and although there may be kind people nearby, the loneliness of existence is ever there. When you face the final journey to your destiny, it is alone that those footsteps are taken. No one can go there with you. All memory of the past is wiped clean - the slate cleared for the new start as a woman. It is not a romantic dream, or the drag queen's glittering finery, but cold reality. You have set yourself free, but the social turmoil of a new life, work and relationships with the new 'opposite sex', in all its variations, is to come. In thanks to the surgeons, I can only say, in the words of Pink Floyd, from The Dark Side of the Moon:

'You raise the blade, and take away the pain,
you rearrange me till I'm sane.'

Joy

Appendices

Appendix 1. Joy's Post Script

Joy: Now the nightmare of confusion is over I can, at last, be happy that Joy is here, not having to hide any more from the jeering, prying, cruel world. When this world tries to humiliate me, I stand aloof and untouchable, and say to myself, Joy, you have had to fight for all that life has given you, and only you know how high that price was. I will never forget all my sisters in life. Every woman has been a sister to me; good or bad, they have shown me the way to myself.

Joy: I don't know if this small account of our suffering helps in the cold hard world of today, but if any of you feel the pain of what is before you, if any of you who read this account feel the driving need as we have, then I say to you: cry when you must, and go the way you feel to be right, but be honest and don't hide from the truth of yourself. Make the sacrifices, for at the end of it all, beyond the reach of public humiliation and ridicule laced with an ignorance as old as the sexes themselves, you will find within your soul a peace that you thought could never exist, a forever peace and a gentle face.

Joy: Jan and I spent my first Christmas as Joy together and although he never knew how I felt about him, it was a lovely feeling to have him there in the house to cook and care for, and it gave me the greatest satisfaction to watch him eat the food that I had prepared for him with love. I could at last be myself with him, as feminine as I wanted to be, and he would sit absorbed as I applied my make-up and put on some pretty dress for his approval. The barriers were all down, and he could see the real me that had been shut in for so many years, a me he had seen something of twenty years before. He is my dearest friend, and although I know that we shall never be together in this life, we will be together for all eternity. From the last biscuit to the Christmas dinner, we have maintained contact, and I have loved him.

Joy: Ethical and legal questions continued to cause controversy. Should we be able to marry the now opposite sex? Should our retirement age change? Should we, as new women, be able to join the clergy? Our rights in society are very few at the time of writing. In 1989, we in the UK could not marry a man, because we were still men in the eyes of the law, and under the law in this country, a man could not marry a man. Conversely, I could not stay married to my wife, because I was now a new woman, and a woman could not marry a woman. There was then the question of our birth certificates. The authorities maintained that records could not be changed to accommodate our new sex, therefore the fact that we had changed gender was there for all to see, and all had the legal right to see. We did not have a lot of choice whilst in the throes of this massive upheaval. It has been often enough said that there is no choice other than to go on, or commit suicide, and yet we are treated as second class citizens, as though we have committed a crime.

Appendix 2. Joy's Life after Transition
By Sarah Connor

Joy transitioned in 1989 and lived a happy life, although she always had a haunted look, due to her traumatic past. Ironically, it wasn't until she suffered from dementia in her last years that she looked truly happy, her expression one of a person at peace. Loss of memory meant she was finally free of the burdens she had carried for so long.

She shared the rest of her life with her friend, Mary, and had a relationship with a man for thirty five years, as a partner and later as a good friend, until she died in 2019. Joy never stopped travelling, going to Holland and Greece with Mary, in search of work as nurses and to make a fresh start. They lived in France for a few years, renovating a cottage, eventually returning to the UK to settle on a houseboat in Gloucestershire. Joy always loved animals, keeping many cats and dogs as pets over the years, including Charlie, a Yorkshire terrier, who appeared in a Plymouth newspaper with her in the nineteen eighties.

Joy was skilled at everything she turned her hand to, including cabinet making, upholstery, dressmaking and taxidermy. She spent ten years researching and documenting the history of glass making, producing a fourteen volume encyclopaedia used by the Society of Glass Technology. Her life story is a legacy for others experiencing gender dysphoria, and for their families and friends. Joy's spirit was unbreakable. She was the bravest, strongest, most extraordinary person I have ever known.

Appendix 3. A Personal Perspective
By Sarah Connor

From my experience as an adult involved with a trans support group, I now realise that my mum and I were those family members discussed in the group, who make it more difficult for members to move on with their new lives and identities. But when my dad left us and became Karen, followed by Joy, I was fourteen and just wanted my dad back, not this stranger that he now was to me. My mum and I were confused and angry.

I know now that she was struggling to leave her past behind and that I was dragging her back to something she didn't want to remember. She saw herself completely detached from Frederick and despised the man that she had been. I guess, in a way, it's a bit like having a split personality.

As is the case with many children in difficult family situations, I felt a deep sadness and the need to support and protect my parents. I had the best childhood you could wish for, and we were a very close family. I stuck by my dad and tried to help Joy adjust to her new life and learn how to behave like a woman and how to cook, amongst other things.

I moved away to Germany for twelve years, from the age of nineteen, and our relationship during that time was not always a good one. We had fallen into a strange pattern of reversed parent / child roles. I was still the person who listened to Joy's problems, often very personal things that I was not equipped to deal with. It felt like I had become the adult in the relationship, and it took its toll on me. Every time I had a letter or a phone call from her, I was extremely upset afterwards. There were so many things she did and opinions she had that I disagreed with, and I just didn't want to hear about any of it anymore. Eventually, I said that I needed a complete break from all forms of contact. This hurt us both immensely, but I had to do it for my own sake.

Of course, deep down, I still wanted her to be my dad. It took me until I was in my forties to accept that I couldn't have him back, and it felt like he had died, but he was actually still alive, he just wasn't my dad anymore. I spent years grieving for the loss, before finally embracing the new person he was - Joy. I realised that this was a person just trying to make the best of the life they had been given. As a child I idolised my dad and I carried that with me into adulthood, along with high expectations. Knowing his history, I later realised what a damaged person he was and how much he struggled with being a parent to me. He had little guidance as a child and made his own way in the world. It was I who eventually taught him about the boundaries between parent and child and what my expectations were of a father. In her later years, I caught more and more glimpses of the person I recognised and loved. I never loved Joy, but always knew my dad was still in there somewhere, along with his memories.

The majority of people who transition now do so at a younger age, which is great. It took my dad until he was forty, and he had a wife and child, which makes my perspective rather unique. I know that many family members struggle or refuse to use the correct pronoun and that this is very distressing for the person concerned; however, there was no way for me to change the fact that she was my dad. I was always respectful and used her name and her female pronoun in company, but when we were alone, she agreed I could still call her 'daddy', and signed letters 'from your dad'. It became more complex in later life when she had to be admitted to a care home, with dementia. I then had to refer to her as my mother, as it would have been far too complicated to do anything else. My last words to her after she died were, 'Goodbye Daddy'.

I first read her life story in my mid forties, and had to skip quite a few parts as I couldn't bear to read them. But I did read it again in more detail, and realised the potential it had to help others understand what compels people to change their gender. Joy had tried to publish the story herself, without success. Unfortunately, it wasn't until she passed away in October 2019, that I made contact with a publisher who was interested. I know how happy and proud she would be that it is finally out there. She lived an incredibly interesting life and I am glad I have an account of it and have been part of her story.

Appendix 4. LGBT in Joy's Lifetime: Beliefs, Rights and Laws in the UK
Reviewed by Sarah Connor

Beliefs, rights and laws around persons within the LGBT community changed significantly during the time that Joy was alive. When she was born in 1945, there was little or no understanding around identifying as another gender or being homosexual, and it was seen as a disease or mental illness. In 1946, Michael Dillon published Self: A Study in Endocrinology. This is the autobiography of the first transgender man to undergo phalloplasty surgery, telling of his journey from Laura to Michael, and the surgeries undertaken by pioneering surgeon Sir Harold Gillies. Dillon wrote: 'Where the mind cannot be made to fit the body, the body should be made to fit, approximately at any rate, to the mind' (LGB+T History, challenges and successes, 2012).

It wasn't until 1951 that Roberta Cowell underwent male-to-female confirmation surgery, a first in Britain. But being homosexual was against the law after WWII and there was a rise in arrests and prosecutions of gay men. Many were from high rank and held positions within government and national institutions, such as Alan Turing, the cryptographer whose work played a decisive role in the breaking of the Enigma code (News.bbc.co.uk, 2009).

This increase in prosecutions called into question the legal system in place for dealing with homosexual acts.

It was only in 1967 that the Government implemented the Sexual Offences Act, which partially legalised same-sex acts in the UK between men over the age of twenty-one, conducted in private. Scotland and Northern Ireland didn't follow suit until 1980 and 1981 respectively (Pidd, 2010). The Sexual Offences Act represented a stepping stone towards equality, but there was still a long way to go.

This meant that during her early years and well into Joy's twenties, there was little information about gender dysphoria, and the gay sex she was having with men was illegal and could have landed her in jail. It is likely that she was discharged from the army because they suspected she was homosexual.

When she finally realised what was going on and came out as Karen in the nineteen eighties, homosexuality was no longer a criminal offence, nor considered an illness, but there was still a lot of hostility and prejudice against the LGBT community and little was still known by most, about transgender persons. It took until 2002 for the government to formally recognise that transsexualism is not a mental illness (Department for Constitutional Affairs, 2002).

Transgender is an umbrella term used to include people whose lifestyles appear to conflict with the gender norms of society (En.wikipedia.org, 2001). A transgender person crosses the conventional boundaries of gender; in clothing; in presenting themselves; even as far as having multiple surgical procedures to be fully bodily reassigned in their preferred gender role. There have been three categories generally used to describe trans people – transvestite, transgender and transsexual, however trans-people often have complex gender identities, and may move from one 'trans' category into another over time (GLAAD, n.d.).

During the nineteen eighties and nineties, things finally started to change, and in 1980, a British documentary 'A Change of Sex', aired on BBC 2, enabled viewers to follow the social and medical transition of Julia Grant. The Self Help Association for Transsexuals (SHAFT) was formed as an information collecting and disseminating body for trans-people. The association later became known as 'Gender Dysphoria Trust International' (GDT) (Dixon, 1993).

Anti-discrimination measures have existed since 1999 and were strengthened in the two thousands, to include anti-harassment wording. Later, in 2010, gender reassignment was included as a protected characteristic in the Equality Act. The Marriage (same sex couples) Act 2013 made it possible for a spouse to legally change their gender without requiring a divorce, in mainland UK (The Marriage (Same Sex Couples) Act 2013: The Equality and Human Rights Implications for Marriage and the Law in England and Wales, 2014).

Despite changes in the law, I remember Joy reporting that she was often verbally abused and threatened with violence – once by two men in a car, with a baseball bat. Unfortunately, trans women face difficulties for many years of their life as they struggle with the limitations of medicine and surgery to pass as ordinary women in their day to day life. They are more likely than trans men to become victims of transphobia and to experience the social stigmatisation that comes with it. As in Joy's case, many trans women who eventually live in their acquired gender will face an unpleasant divorce and the loss of family home, access to children, and financial problems associated with it. This adds further burdens to their transition (Whittle, Turner and Al-Alimi, 2007).

The growth of home computer use in the nineteen nineties, and internet development, has meant that although geographically spread out, people are no longer isolated. There is a trans community with an understanding and awareness of common experiences, and the increasing media coverage of trans stories relating to inequalities and discrimination has broadened people's minds and helped LGBT persons become more accepted in wider society. It is also a platform from which people can learn the legal mechanisms which can be used to claim 'rights', as well as the pathway they need to follow to start their journey of transformation (Whittle, Turner and Al-Alimi, 2007).

Despite many improvements, the NHS is not always a welcoming place for many trans people (Curtis et al., 2014). Treatment is often only obtained as a result of a huge struggle past GPs, nursing staff and psychiatrists, to be met with the news that there are very few surgeons and the waiting list is several years long.

Unsurprisingly, the figures for attempted suicide or self harm, due to social attitudes and reactions, are high (Public Health England & The Royal College of Nursing, 2015). I know Joy contemplated killing herself, my mother and me at one point, to spare us the pain that was to come, and survived taking an overdose with her friend, Mary, in the nineteen nineties.

In 2004, The Gender Recognition Act 2004 was passed. This gave transsexual people legal recognition as members of the sex appropriate to their gender (male or female) allowing them to acquire a new birth certificate, giving them full recognition of their acquired sex in law for all purposes, including marriage. The equality acts of 2006 and 2007 provided legal protection against discrimination with regards to the provision of goods and services. Although there was still a lot of prejudice, this meant people had legal rights with which to contest it.

Things have moved on a lot since then, possibly with the help of social media, which has enabled a wider audience to access information. There are forty LGBT MPs in the UK Parliament, which in 2016 was the most in any parliament around the world (Hooper, 2016). In 2017, Andy Street became the United Kingdom's first openly gay, directly elected metro mayor (Butterworth, 2017). Philippa York, formerly Robert Millar, became the first former professional cyclist to have publicly transitioned (Fotheringham, 2017). In 2019, Laverne Cox was one of fifteen women chosen by guest editor Meghan, Duchess of Sussex, to appear on the cover of the September 2019 issue of British Vogue (Barr 2019), and Songs of Praise showed its first gay wedding (Dixon, 2019). Lucia Lucas became the first transgender singer to perform with the English National Opera in London (Lucia Lucas: Making UK operatic debut at the ENO, 2019).

The singular pronoun 'they/them' was announced as word of the year 2019, according to Merriam-Webster, giving gender-neutral pronouns much-needed recognition (Merriam-Webster names "they" its word of the year, 2019). The pronoun is most prominently used by non-binary people across the UK, allowing people to be referred to without being gendered as 'she' or 'he'. We have also seen a wider array of positive media representation, with TV shows such as Pose and Butterfly accurately reflecting the experiences of transgender people. A growing number of influential individuals are showing their support for transgender people and trans youth publicly, including Jameela Jamil, Prince Harry, Alexandria Ocasio-Cortez and Harry Brewer. Emma Watson has shown staunch support for young people who are transgender (Owl, 2020).

Had Joy been born in the 21st century, her life might have been a lot easier. Children and young people are now recognised as transgender at an earlier age and hormone blockers can be prescribed in the UK to over 16s if the person meets the criteria. These don't have any long term effect, but they 'pause' puberty, so that the body doesn't start to develop in a male or female way until the person has time and support to think things through. Puberty is the release of sex hormones by either the testes or the ovaries, which leads to a range of bodily changes, including growth of pubic hair and hair on the legs, armpits, development of breasts and increase in size of the testes and penis, the beginning of periods or erections and 'wet dreams'(Whittle, Turner and Al-Alimi, 2007).

For young people who are experiencing gender dysphoria, puberty can often be a time of increased distress as their body develops differently to that which is in line with their gender identity. In 2020, this is the point at which they seek a referral to GIDS (Gender Identity Development Service).

References

Barr, S. (29 July 2019). "Meghan Markle: Jameela Jamil, Laverne Cox and Gemma Chan react to appearing on cover of British Vogue". The Independent. Yahoo! News.

News.bbc.co.uk. (2009). BBC NEWS | Technology | PM apology after Turing petition. [online] Available at: http://news.bbc.co.uk/1/hi/technology/8249792.stm [Accessed 5 Mar. 2020].

Merriam-Webster names "they" its word of the year. (2019). BBC News. [online] 10 Dec. Available at: https://www.bbc.co.uk/news/world-us-canada-50735371 [Accessed 8 Mar. 2020].

Lucia Lucas: Making UK operatic debut at the ENO, (2019). [interview] BBC. 5 Aug. Available at: https://www.bbc.co.uk/news/video_and_audio/headlines/499 43671/lucia-lucas-making-uk-operatic-debut-at-the-eno [Accessed 8 Mar. 2020].

Butterworth, B. (2017). Conservative Andy Street becomes UK's first directly-elected gay metro mayor. Pink News. [online] Available at: https://www.pinknews.co.uk/2017/05/05/gay-conservative-andy-street-elected-metro-mayor-of-west-midlands/ [Accessed 5 Mar. 2020].

Curtis, R., Levy, A., Martin, J., Playdon, Z., Wylie, K., Reed, T. and Reed, B. (2014). A Guide to Trans Service Users' Rights– Legal Aspects; NHS Funding Processes and Waiting Times; Pursuing Appeals and Complaints; Service User Involvement in the NHS. [ebook] Gires. Available at: https://www.gires.org.uk/wp-content/uploads/2014/10/trans-rights.pdf [Accessed 5 Mar. 2020].

Department for Constitutional Affairs (2002).
https://web.archive.org/web/20080511211217/http://www.
dca.gov.uk/constitution/transsex/policy.htm.

Dixon, H. (2019). Songs of Praise broadcasts show's first gay wedding. The Telegraph. [online] Available at:
https://www.telegraph.co.uk/news/2019/08/18/songs-praise-broadcasts-shows-first-gay-wedding/ [Accessed 5 Mar. 2020].

Dixon, S. (1993). "Dixon, Stephen Michael (1993) Gender dysphoria: Transsexualism and identity. Masters thesis, Durham University" (PDF). 1993.

Fotheringham, W. (2017). Philippa York: 'I've known I was different since I was a five-year-old'. The Guardian.

GLAAD. (2016). GLAAD Media Reference Guide - Transgender. 10th Edition [PDF] Available at:
https://www.glaad.org/sites/default/files/GLAAD-Media-Reference-Guide-Tenth-Edition.pdf [Accessed 5 Mar. 2020].

Gender Identity Development Service . Puberty and physical intervention | GIDS. [online] gids.nhs.uk. Available at:
https://gids.nhs.uk/puberty-and-physical-intervention.

Hooper, M. (2016). The UK has more LGBT MPs than anywhere else in the world. Gay Times.

LGB+T History, challenges and successes. (2012). 2nd ed. the Equality and Diversity Team, NHS North West, Page 12.

Owl (2020). In 2020, let's end the needless hostility towards trans people. [online] Metro. Available at:
https://metro.co.uk/2020/01/01/2020-lets-end-needless-hostility-towards-trans-people-11982365 [Accessed 8 Mar. 2020].

Pidd, H. (2010). Pride 2010: From section 28 to Home Office float, Tories come out in force. [online] the Guardian. Available at: https://www.theguardian.com/world/2010/jul/02/tories-out-in-force-gay-pride [Accessed 5 Mar. 2020].

Public Health England & The Royal College of Nursing (2015). Preventing suicide among trans young people A toolkit for nurses.

The Marriage (Same Sex Couples) Act 2013: The Equality and Human Rights Implications for Marriage and the Law in England and Wales. (2014). Equality and Human Rights Commission.

Whittle, S., Turner, L. and Al-Alimi, M. (2007). Engendered Penalties: Transgender and Transsexual People's Experiences of Inequality and Discrimination. [ebook] Manchester Metropolitan University. Available at: http://www.pfc.org.uk/pdf/EngenderedPenalties.pdf [Accessed 5 Mar. 2020].

En.wikipedia.org. (2001). Transgender. [online] Available at: https://en.wikipedia.org/wiki/Transgender [Accessed 5 Mar. 2020].